Women & Power

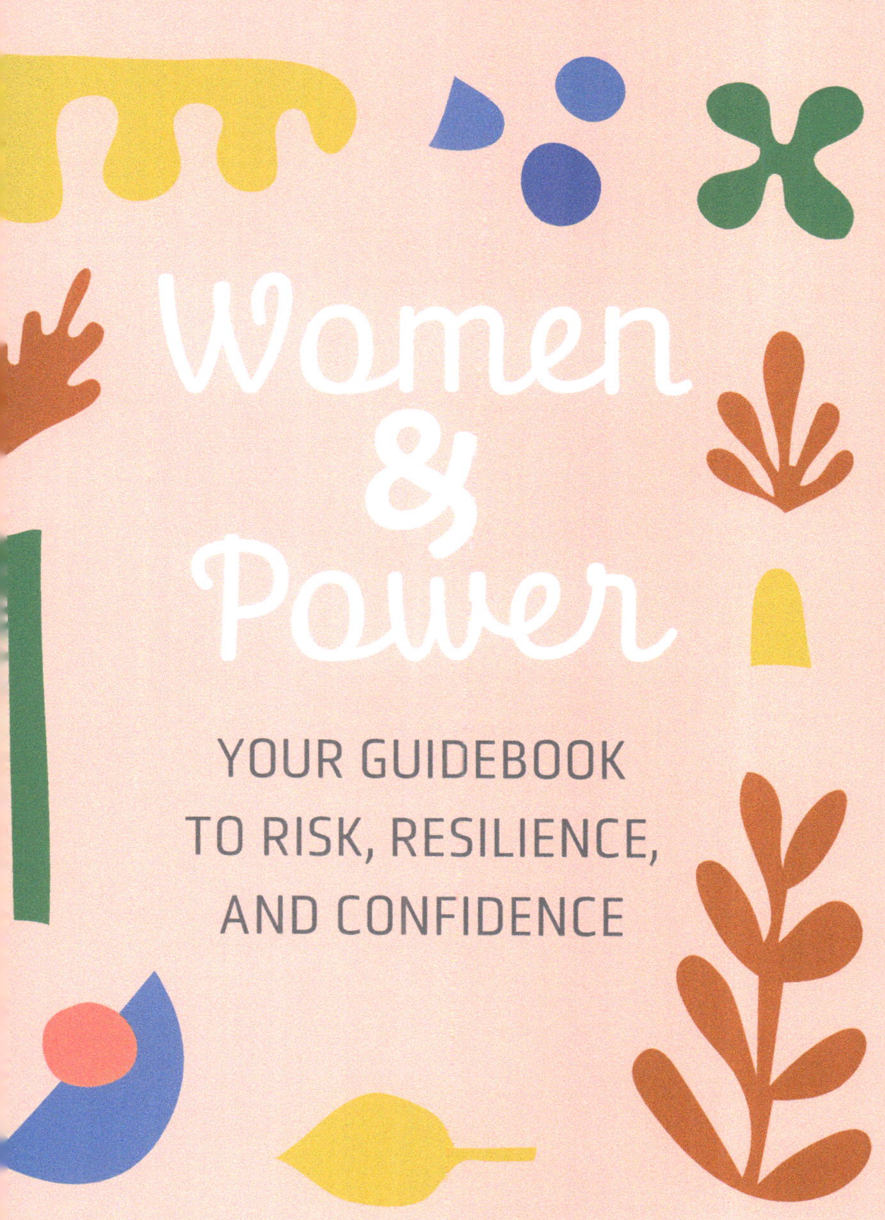

Women & Power

YOUR GUIDEBOOK TO RISK, RESILIENCE, AND CONFIDENCE

JANE ZIEGLER SOJKA

About the University of Cincinnati Press

The University of Cincinnati Press is committed to publishing rigorous, peer-reviewed, leading scholarship accessibly to stimulate dialog between the academy, public intellectuals and lay practitioners. The Press endeavors to erase disciplinary boundaries to cast fresh light on common problems in our global community. Building on the university's longstanding tradition of social responsibility to the citizens of Cincinnati, the state of Ohio, and the world, the press publishes books on topics that expose and resolve disparities at every level of society and have a local, national, and global impact.

The University of Cincinnati Press, Cincinnati 45221
Copyright © 2025

Library of Congress Control Number:
2024950213

ISBN 978-1-947603-73-8 (paperback)
ISBN 978-1-947603-74-5 (e-book, PDF)
ISBN 978-1-947603-75-2 (e-book, EPUB)

Designed and produced for UC Press by Julie Rushing
Typeset in: Finlay and Obvia
Printed in the United States of America

DEDICATION

This book is dedicated to the young women with whom I work and to my family.

To the young women who encouraged me, tested me, pushed me, and showed up every day with their enthusiasm, their youthfulness, and their brilliance. You have given me the best career I could ever imagine. I hope you learned as much from me as I learned from you.

To my family—Greg, Laura, Ann, and Joan. Each of you sacrificed to make this book possible and allowed me to pursue my dream. You are the best family ever and I love you all.

CONTENTS

ACKNOWLEDGMENTS

It takes a village to raise a child, and it took a village to produce this book. This book would not have been possible without the constant support and encouragement from my friend and department head, Dr. Karen Machleit and her boss, Dr. Marianne Lewis. These two women supported, promoted, and protected me while I was developing this material. Thank you both for believing in my crazy idea and for supporting me all along the way. This book couldn't have been written without the opportunities you encouraged me to pursue. Thank you.

I am in deep gratitude to my friend and colleague Dr. Donna Chrobot-Mason who graciously hired me, a marketer by trade, to lead the women's initiatives in the Warren Bennis Leadership Institute. Thanks to Donna's support, this book was moved from a dream to a work priority for the Institute. Donna made sure other obligations didn't deter me from writing, and for that I am grateful.

The young women I mentor and coach were essential in helping me test ideas, activities, and concepts as I experimented with the material, learned what worked, and uncovered what else was needed. It is impossible to name the hundreds of participants—young women and men—who experimented with me to develop the content. There are, however, several special women who need to be named.

Hannah Markel, a former mentee, was instrumental in prodding me to start putting the fifteen-week-for-credit-course into a book and workshop format. Her passion for the project never wavered, and her guidance and encouragement gave me the determination to continually move forward. Korina Wray and Katie Ryder (former mentees gifted in graphic design) provided the creativity and design expertise on the preliminary drafts that formed the foundation for the current conceptualization.

Many thanks to Emily McDonough, another mentee, who inspired me to dream about possibilities for women and gave me to courage to keep fighting. While Emily and I didn't get the women's wing in the new building that we proposed, together we kept women's issues in the forefront of our organization and with the appointment of Dr. Marianne Lewis, have made remarkable strides for women.

The quality of this manuscript was greatly enhanced by Elizabeth (Lizzy) Geraghty's initial edits and graphic design. As my assistant and eventual mentee, Lizzy assured me that I did have an important message and that it was conveyed in a format and style that would reach young women and beyond. I knew the manuscript was good when Lizzy liked it.

And I would be remiss if I didn't mention Jessica (Jess) Davis, another former mentee. While not intimately involved in the manuscript text per se, Jess reminded me of the importance of getting this information in writing and available to a wider audience. Women shouldn't have to take a fifteen-week-for-credit-course to learn to get over their fear of failure, practice resilience, and build confidence. The opportunity to learn those skills should be available to every woman and Jess reminded me of that the entire year we worked together. There are literally thousands of other former young women who helped shape this book and the material in it who cannot be named. But know that you all contributed to its content and its success.

This book would not have been possible without the help from everyone at the University of Cincinnati Press. I am indebted to Elizabeth (Liz) Scarpelli—for her constant encouragement, belief in the subject matter, and confidence in my writing ability. Liz, your editorial expertise and publishing knowledge made this a smooth and enjoyable process. Many thanks to Nick Thompson for his careful eye and gentle edits. I could not have managed the electronic version without the help and expertise of Mark Minelli. And a special note of thanks to Pamela Wissman whose imagination and gift for visuals made my words come alive. It was truly a joy to work with all of you.

Finally, I cannot thank my family—Greg Sojka, Laura Wilson, Ann Sojka, and Joan Gwizdak—enough for their support and encouragement of this project. To my husband Greg, who saw far more potential in me than I saw in myself. When the rest of the world saw a stay-at-home mom, you saw a PhD and prospective leader. Thank you for making all this happen. To my precious daughters who taught me so much and who, no surprise, all ended up in predominately male industries. When I watched each of you battle the exact same issues I thought we had won forty years ago, I knew I had to enter the women's movement again. I'm so proud of each of you for standing your ground and not giving up. Together we are building a strong foundation for the next generation. Best family ever.

Thank you all.

HOW TO USE THIS BOOK

How many of you negotiated your first job? If you did, good for you. Stop reading and get a refund on this book. Full disclosure: I didn't negotiate my first job. Or my second job. Or even the job I have now. I thought it was a miracle they wanted to hire me. But now I negotiate everything because it's never too late. So, if you're like me, and like most women, keep reading. You need what I needed and what we'll be working on throughout this text: getting over your fear of failure, practicing resilience, and cultivating confidence. And for the record, if you didn't negotiate your first job, you're in good company. According to research by Linda Babcock, turns out only 7% of women ask for more than what they are offered. We need this book.

Does the title of this book scare you? No worries. The thought of women and power used to scare me too. So much so that I was afraid to put the two words—women and power—together. Take a deep breath and hang with me here. Why was I afraid to associate with power, much less claim my own? I had seen power terribly misused—power over people, not shared power with people—and the last thing I ever wanted to do was be a tyrant and hold power over people. But that's not what this book is about. This gentle guidebook is about helping you learn how to claim your own power so that your competence shines through and isn't squashed by a lack of confidence. As a young woman I was mentoring said, "I had my voice all along and I was conditioned not to use it." We have our voices and our expertise; now is time to learn the confidence to use that expertise without fear and self-doubt. You can be strong and compassionate, and you can be powerful and kind; the two are not mutually exclusive. This guidebook is designed to help you bring out the best of you. You are likely already compassionate and kind; it's time to learn how to be strong and powerful. How do you change the world? One woman at a time. And as we claim our power and strength and share it with others, the world will change.

Before we go too much further and you invest your precious time and energy reading and practicing the ideas in this book, let me offer this disclaimer about what this book is not. This book does not attempt to explain, justify, or even propose reasons why women tend to be more worried about failure than men, or have less resilience and less confidence than men. I have my suspicions, but assigning causality to the issues we will be discussing is beyond my expertise and the scope of this book. I'll leave causal explanations to other researchers. I coach future business leaders and what I can do is help you learn behaviors and thought patterns that will help you overcome your fear of failure, practice resilience, and build confidence. What I can't explain is how we got this way in the first place.

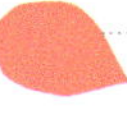

If you want to change the world, change yourself.

In addition, I am all too much aware of the many barriers intentionally and unintentionally designed to undermine women's power. Life is not fair and that statement is especially true for women. But this I know. I cannot personally change the government, laws, society, culture, religious institutions, educational institutions, or even other people. And believe me, in my younger, rebellious protest years, I tried. It didn't work and all I got was beat up. I acknowledge that there are external forces that need to be changed if women are to thrive. A business colleague once commented that I am "changing the world, one business leader at a time" and it stuck. I may not be able to change the world (darn!) but I can change myself and that change will have a ripple effect that will eventually change the world—one person at a time. When one of us has the courage to speak up, it empowers more of us to speak up and that leads to change.

This book is a culmination of what I have learned, practiced, and observed about women and power. It's about getting over your fear of failure and learning how to take risks. It's about practicing resilience to acknowledge that failure isn't the end of the journey, it's just a temporary setback. And it's about building confidence that you are good enough—not perfect—but good enough to succeed at your position, to speak up in a meeting, and to ask for what you want. I am passionate about communicating these topics, not because I was an expert when I started, but because I needed to learn them and women in predominately male industries need to learn them too.

WHY DID I WRITE THIS BOOK?

The material in this book is an outgrowth of an innovation grant from Proctor & Gamble. Frustrated with the miniscule number of women entering the lucrative and career building field of professional selling, I began experimenting with a course in sales designed for women. When I started the course, all I knew was that women sold differently than men. Not better. Not worse. Differently. And I saw value in those differences. The first class consisted of twenty-five women and two men—men have always been welcomed in the course and they become our biggest allies—and was offered in the spring of 2015. It didn't take long for me to see the gender gap in skills critical for success in sales: courage to take a risk, resilience if you get turned down, and confidence to ask for what you want. Word among women quickly spread and what I thought would be a one-time only experiment has sent me down a path of empowering women that I never expected or predicted. Over 240 women every year are exposed to this material with over 1,400 women having completed the course. And there is no intention of slowing down.

A woman whom I mentored, who was also a varsity college athlete, helped me realize that the skills, habits, and mindset shifts being taught had applications far greater than the professional sales industry. An empowerment program for women athletes, –Inspire, Equip, Connect– was born from a summer collaboration with my mentee. Together, we transformed the women's empowerment pieces of the sales course into a fun, engaging workshop to help women athletes get comfortable with their power. This book is an outgrowth of that program and is the written version of the Inspire, Equip, Connect women's empowerment program still in use by university women athletes.

HOW THIS BOOK IS DESIGNED

This book is designed for you, to fit your needs. You can read it straight through cover to cover—like a traditional book. But if you're starved for time like most of us, you can also skip around to the topics that interest you, or scare you, the most.

Think of it like a cookbook, which is ironic because I do not cook, I do not like to cook, nor am I good at cooking. But I know how to use a cookbook to manage a dinner, side dish, or dessert when the occasion arises. Hence, instead of reading the topics in order, you can pick and choose and start with the issues that you struggle with the most. Try what you need. Skip around. Read and practice the activities for handling risk, practicing resilience, and building confidence in the order that suits you.

I never cease to be amazed at the order that other women have chosen when addressing the topics in this book. As part of the process of developing this book, I led several groups of women, over the course of five years, through the material contained in the book, with the women athletes choosing the topics they wanted and needed to cover. The first cohort wanted to start with "Women Supporting Women: Finding Your Fan Girls." The second group started with "Progress Over Perfection." The third group started with the "Sorry, I'm Not Sorry" section. That's not the order I would choose. And that's OK. Each group chose the order that resonated with them, and you have my permission to do the same. Start practicing what *you* need to learn.

This book can be used in a variety of capacities. You can use it in a group setting—like we do in the Inspire, Equip, & Connect women's empowerment workshops—and use the reflection questions to generate group discussions. The reflection questions are equally suitable for small or larger group discussions. The practice steps are fun to try and then report back to the group what happened. This book is designed to generate reflection, discussion, and practice.

But if you're an introvert like me and prefer working alone, or you don't have a group to join, no problem. You can work through the book on your own. We purposefully left room in the margins for you to make notes and write down your reactions to the questions. Whichever way you choose to digest this material—with a group or by yourself—I have confidence that it will be the right way for you.

In each part, there are places for you to pause and reflect. This can be a group discussion or a time to journal. In addition, practice exercises are included to help you gain confidence in your skills. As I learned from working in business, "You don't learn to sell from reading about it in a textbook. You learn to sell by practicing selling." The same is true for building confidence. You build confidence in your abilities by practicing the skill set in safe settings while slowly and intentionally raising the level of risk. Practice the activities and see what happens. I'm excited to be on this self-discovery journey with you.

FINAL THOUGHTS AS WE BEGIN OUR JOURNEY

One of my favorite quotations is that "when the student is ready, the teacher will appear." I must have been ready, because over 1,400 teachers have appeared in the form of women (and some good men) who trusted me to coach them as they pursued careers in predominately male industries and subsequently taught me what they needed to learn. Although I studied gender differences in selling as part of my doctoral dissertation, and I knew that women tended to be good at building relationships—a critical capability in sales—I didn't know much else about gender differences. As I slowly got to know these thousands of women trying to build their careers in predominantly male industries, I saw the gender gap in risk, resilience, and confidence, and started experimenting with activities to narrow those educational gaps. And it worked. It changed the women, and it changed me. Something magical happens when you get women together and this book is living proof. My work with closing the gender gap in confidence changed the trajectory of my career and this book is the outgrowth of that journey. I dedicate this book to all the people—women and men—who made the content in this book possible. Thank you.

INTRODUCTION

Here's the scenario. Think about a job application—for a new position at a new company or for a different position at your existing company. A job posting typically lists the criteria the manager is looking for in the job candidates. Typical postings will want the applicant to have certain degrees, experience, time in grade, certifications etc. etc. etc. Suppose you are reading the job posting. The job sounds exciting—something you've always wanted or in a location where you've always wanted to live or someone or some company you've always dreamed about working for. In other words, you'd like to get this job. You have some of the criteria mentioned in the job posting, but not all. Would you apply? Or in more general terms, what percentage of the job posting criteria does the average applicant need to have before they will apply for the position? Spoiler alert: This is trick question, and the results aren't pretty. And for the record, if I didn't meet most of the criteria, I wouldn't apply.

In an oft-cited, now-infamous study, Hewlett-Packard asked its employees that same question. The results were stunning to me, but not surprising to human resources managers who are accustomed to receiving job applications. Their research showed that if men met 60% of the desired criteria, they would apply for the position. Whoa! Wait a minute and let me get this straight. Men, who have only a little more than half of the desired criteria—60%—have the audacity to apply for a position where they lacked almost half of the qualifications. Seriously?!? And to be fair, good for them. I don't want to squash their ambition.

But the results for women take my breath away. As you might have guessed, the results for women were equally dramatic, but discouraging. What percentage, on average, do women feel they need to have before applying for a position? 100%. That's right. 100%. We must be perfect. And that's before we even apply for the job. How much more pressure for perfection do we demand of ourselves once we get the position? (Hint: see section on perfectionism.)

If you don't ask, the answer is always no.

What's the big deal? Why does this statistic bother me so much? How do you spell "lose?" That's right. If this statistic is correct—and based on my experience and observation, I have no reason to doubt it—when women don't take a risk and apply, we all lose. When we hold ourselves back from taking a risk and applying—or fail to "lean in" as Sheryl Sandburg eloquently notes—organizations lose, and women lose.

Let's be magnanimous and think about the impact of this research on the well-being of the company first. How would you feel if you were a manager and an individual with 60% of the suggested attributes applied for the job, but someone with 80% of the criteria doesn't apply because she isn't perfectly 100% qualified? If I were the manager, I'd be frustrated. In the words of an old AT&T commercial, 80% is better than 60%. The company loses when we hold ourselves back because we feel unqualified if we're not perfect.

But the real reason this statistic bothers me so much is what it says about us—we pull ourselves out of the game before we even start. Because of our fear of failure, rather than risk rejection, we don't even apply. And if you don't ask, the answer is always no.

CONFESSIONS FROM THE QUEEN OF FAILURE

Let me show you how this misguided quest for perfection and fear of failure and rejection has played out in my life and the lives of other women. Several years ago, I found myself in a tenure-track position at a reputable university. For those of you not familiar with academia, tenure is the gold standard; the prize that we are taught to strive for from the beginning of our first doctoral seminar. Tenure was an apex of an academic career in terms of stability, respect, and salary. And as you might guess, tenure is not easy to come by, and part of the academic hazing process is scaring the heck out of untenured faculty. Believe me, my colleagues at a former institution did a good job of that. In fact, I was so afraid that I would not get tenure, I went to the head of my department and suggested that I would like to step down from a tenure-track position and instead teach part-time for the university. Whoa! Wait a minute! Are you kidding me?!? Get this straight. I was so afraid that I might not get tenure, that I was ready to pull myself out of the opportunity, rather than risk the possibility of failure or rejection. BTW—The thought I might be successful and earn tenure never crossed my mind. I was so afraid of being rejected and failing, I decided to pull myself out of contention rather than take the chance that someone else would tell me no. Talk about fear of failure; I was its poster child.

Fortunately for me, my story has a happy ending. The chair of my department—a kind and wise man—sat me down and reminded me of my accomplishments. I had the teaching evaluations, the publications, and the service needed to earn tenure. And he was right. I was tenured at that school and the rest is history.

But relaying my experiences to women made it clear that I was not alone in my fear of failure or rejection and the limitations I put on myself to avoid that possibility. One by one, women shared similar stories about how they held themselves back from pursuing opportunities—internships, jobs, promotions, organizational offices, etc. etc. etc.—because they were afraid of rejection or failure. One of my favorite examples came from a former high school basketball player. Raised as a Hoosier, I have watched enough basketball to know that when men shoot the ball and miss, they keep right on shooting—whether they have an open shot or not. Drives me, and the coach, crazy. This woman did the exact opposite. When she missed a shot, she was so distraught, she called for the coach to take her out of the game. Rather than take a chance on missing the basket again—failure—she literally pulled herself out of the game. While these are my examples, I'm sure you have similar scenarios that have played out in dorm rooms, apartments, homes, and even penthouse suites. How many jobs (they wouldn't want me), teams (I'm not good enough), leadership positions (it's a popularity contest and I'm not popular), elections (I wouldn't get elected), have you *not* applied for? Fear is paralyzing and fear of failure is no different. Fear of failure is paralyzing. It prevents us from taking risks and pursuing opportunities. If you don't shoot the basketball, you'll never score, and if you don't ask, the answer is always no.

Let me be clear. This is not a book about how to *get* what you want. There are plenty of "name it and claim it" books and this is not one of them. This is a book that teaches you how to *ask* for what you want. In the words of that wise sage, Mick Jagger of the Rolling Stones, "You can't always get what you want." But you will *never* get it if you don't ask, and as we all know from cold calling in sales, the more you ask, the more you increase your chances of success. The key is in the asking.

True, there are external factors—prejudice, misogyny, inequity, injustice, and others—that impact whether or not we are treated fairly and get what we want. I can't control the government, society, culture, or even my family for that matter. (And heaven knows, and my husband will attest, for years I tried to control my husband and all it did was make us both miserable.) Many or most external factors are out of my direct control. What I can control, however, are my thoughts, words, and actions. And I can either choose to be a victim, declare a pity party (more on that later), shrivel up, and disappear, or I can choose to continue moving forward with resilience and confidence. Clearly, I choose the latter. This book focuses on changes we can choose to make that I would argue will eventually have a ripple effect in the world. If you want to change the world, start by changing yourself.

Reflect—*Can you think of a time when you chose not to pursue something because you thought you might not get it? A job? Internship? Promotion? Project? What held you back?*

You seldom regret what you do; you regret what you didn't do.

As the self-appointed Queen of Fear, masquerading as college professor and business leader, I started asking women why they were so afraid of taking risks and pursuing opportunities. Their answers did not surprise me. They were afraid of rejection, afraid they might be told no, afraid of disappointing others, afraid of what people would think—in short, afraid of failure and rejection. What did surprise me was that the answers from young women beginning their careers were identical to the same fears I heard voiced by professional women as part of the executive education workshops I teach. Women in high-ranking corporate leadership positions, with years of management experience, expressed the same fears that were paralyzing young women just starting out. Clearly, I am not alone in my struggle with fear of failure and the fear doesn't diminish with age, or experience, or college degrees. Intentional action is needed.

WHY DON'T WE APPLY? (WHAT ARE WE AFRAID OF?)

There are several reasons why we may hesitate to take a risk and apply for something like a new position or job. The Cinderella complex, or an unconscious desire to be taken care of by someone else, might explain some of our hesitation. When I worked in corporate America, I thought that if I was a good girl and did my job, someone would notice me and promote me: like Cinderella, who was recognized by the prince and then rewarded by a move to the castle. Hence, I bought into the false belief that if I was a good girl, remained quiet, didn't call attention to myself and didn't cause trouble, I would get promoted. Like magic. That works great in fairy tales; not so much in real life. Quoting a Taylor Swift song, "Did all the extra credit, then got graded on a curve." Darn.

Another justification to avoid taking a risk and trying something new is that we might be turned down. We might be told no. Now I'm not wild about being told no and I don't like being rejected. But when spelled out in black and white print, it sounds lame to be afraid of a two-letter word: no. And yet, rejection stings deep. So rather than risk rejection, I'll pass on applying. Expanding that rejection even further, my mind goes into overdrive and wonders what will people think of me if they find out I applied and was rejected? Or will people think I am arrogant and prideful by having the audacity to apply for a job while not meeting all 100% of the desired attributes?

All of these self-defeating thoughts swirling around our heads can be summed up in three words: fear of failure. In fact, I would maintain we are so afraid of failing, that we engage in self-limiting behaviors to avoid the possibility that we might fail. Never mind the equally reasonable possibility that we might succeed. No—we focus on the worst—failure. To be fair, the focus on loss rather than gain is standard humankind decision-making, as documented by Kahneman and Tversky. But we women take it a step farther and because we are so afraid of failing, we hold ourselves back from pursuing opportunities that would be advantageous. And face it, there's enough people who want to hold us back; there is no need for us to hold ourselves back.

HOW THIS BOOK IS ORGANIZED

This book is organized into four parts. In Part 1, we identify self-limiting behaviors that we unconsciously use to avoid the possibility of failure. Perfectionism, people-pleasing, control, isolation, busyness, and failure are all behaviors we erroneously believe we can use to avoid failure. Strategies and practices to eliminate these self-limiting behaviors are highlighted. The antidote to fear of failure is resilience: the ability to bounce back quickly after failure. If you know you can recover from a failure and that a mistake isn't the end of the road, the prospect of failing loses its sting and you're willing to take more risks. Part 2 proposes eight resilience strategies for you to practice and use to build confidence that you can move forward in spite of a mishap. Competence, in any field, needs to be communicated—to yourself and to others. Part 3 highlights small adjustments in our body language, writing, and speaking that can have a big impact on our confidence and how others perceive us. Finally, Part 4 talks about how we can support other women and what we all gain from supporting each other.

I am excited to be on this journey with you. But before we start working on positive behaviors—resilience and confidence—we need to take a hard look at how we hold ourselves back by engaging in self-limiting behaviors to avoid the possibility that we might fail. And if it makes you feel better, I've used all of these self-limiting behaviors at various stages of my life. You are not alone. Let's get started.

SELF-LIMITING BEHAVIORS

How much are we afraid of failing? I would maintain, we are so afraid of failure we adopt self-limiting behaviors to avoid (falsely) the possibility that we might fail. I've identified six self-limiting behaviors used to avoid the possibility of failure: perfectionism, people-pleasing, control, isolation, busyness, and fear of failure. The scary thing about these self-limiting behaviors is that they do as they are named: they box us in and restrain us.

If you wait to be perfect, you'll never do anything. If you focus on pleasing others, you'll never please yourself. Want to control everything? Great. But it's exhausting and you will burn yourself out. Or we can isolate ourselves and pretend we don't need help, which only means we fall apart when we do need help. Finally, we limit ourselves through busyness. While we wear it as a badge of honor—gosh, you must be important because you're always so busy—all busyness does is distract us from our true calling and dilute our powerful focus.

The ironic thing about self-limiting behaviors is that we do not need to limit ourselves; there are plenty of people who want to limit our power, reach, strength, and agency. Why the heck then do we limit ourselves??? This leads to a discussion on why we are so afraid of failing. Remember, we use self-limiting behaviors with the misguided notion that they will prevent failure. Spoiler alert: it doesn't work. But think about this—we use these self-limiting behaviors to avoid the possibility that we might fail. What are we so afraid of that we will confine ourselves to non-productive behaviors on the chance that we can sidestep the possibility of failure? Dissecting the failure process and the thoughts, feelings, and activities that go along with the fear of failure—note: it's not the actual failure. It's the possibility of failure that we're afraid of—concludes this section. If it makes you feel better, I've been stuck in each of these self-limiting behaviors at one time or another in my life. And yes, I still lapse into self-limiting behaviors when I'm not intentional about avoiding them. But knowledge is power so becoming aware when we use these self-limiting behaviors is the first step toward healing. Let's get started.

PROGRESS OVER PERFECTIONISM

Hi, my name is Jane, and I'm a recovering perfectionist. Note the active verb choice. I'd like to say I've licked the habit, but alas, I relapse all too often if not careful. And it turns out, I'm not the only woman struggling with perfectionism. If you look at the authors of my favorite *New York Times* bestselling books on the topic, you might think more women struggle with perfectionism than men. While research tends to support the premise that more women struggle with perfectionism than men, my observations lead me to believe that many men struggle with perfectionism as well. Men may not admit the struggle as freely as women, but the struggle is there all the same.

Here's the problem with perfectionism. If you wait to be perfect (Red Alert!!! You will never be perfect!!!) you will never do anything. If you wait until you have all of the qualifications, all of the answers, all of the experience, you will never do anything. Because you will never have everything you think you need to be perfect. Perfectionism is like chasing the horizon; you never get there.

I see this in my office every, single day. Way too often I have a young person—usually a woman but sometimes a man—come to my office asking for advice. They wonder if they should add a second major or a third minor (and I'm not exaggerating here—you know who you are) on top of their five co-ops and three internships, varsity team membership, etc. so they can get a job. Seriously?!? In my forty-plus years of working with sales recruiters across industries, I have yet to see an entry-level applicant eliminated from a sales job because she didn't have the "right" major or enough internship experience. Never. But I have had women miss good opportunities because they didn't feel they had all of the needed qualifications—i.e., they weren't "perfect"—so they didn't apply.

Not only can perfectionism keep us from taking a risk (we have to be perfect and if we fail that myth is broken), it can also keep us from finishing a project or degree. A common joke among academics is, "What do you call the person who wrote the worst dissertation?" When telling this joke, I immediately add, "Don't you dare say, Dr. Sojka—aka me." So, what *do* you call the person who wrote the worst dissertation? Doctor. And when I told this joke to my colleagues in medicine, they responded the same is true for a medical doctor. What do you call the person at the bottom of the medical school class? Doctor. Pretty scary but true. And in the words of a recovering perfectionist, good enough is better than perfect. And in some cases, done is better than good.

My struggle with perfectionism played out when I was completing my PhD in marketing. I had always been an "A" student. In fact, a "B+" was considered failure by me and I went crazy when I missed that 'A' mark. While working on my PhD however, I had three preschool daughters, an hour commute to my graduate program, and a husband who worked sixty hours a week. I had a choice. I could either continue my perfectionist behaviors and drive my family, including myself, crazy, or I could settle for a "B." I learned to take a "B" because all I needed to do was pass the course and my small daughters needed my attention. Thirty-plus years later I can honestly say I made the right decision.

Is letting go of perfectionism easy or fun? No. Did I feel a tinge of pain (OK, it was downright jealousy and envy) when I failed to be nominated for any graduate awards? You bet. I was green with envy for more than a hot minute. However, in my heart, I knew I didn't deserve any awards; I focused my energy on my family and put graduate school as second. And I also knew I had made the right decision and my family survived intact. Perfectionism is way over-rated.

PERFECTIONISM REFRAME

Hi. My name is Jane and I'm a recovering perfectionist. I'm not sure I'll ever totally get over perfectionism, but it no longer has a strong hold on my life. In addition to the many quotations I use to remind myself of the self-limitation perfectionism requires, I've also tried to reframe how I think about perfectionism. What if I had demanded perfectionism and never submitted my dissertation because it wasn't perfect by my standards? I'd still be working on it, or given up, and I would never have made it in business where I impact women on a daily basis. If you don't apply for a job, or promotion, or committee because you meet some, but not all, of the criteria, who loses? Not only do you lose, your organization loses too. When you meet 80% of the criteria but don't apply because you're "not perfect," your organization has to settle for someone with only 60% of the desired attributes. Not good for you or your organization.

Side note. *Every day I go to a barre class. I am twice as old as most the women and there are some moves my body can no longer do. When the instructor tells the class to "go down another inch," I realized that if I go down another inch, I am not getting back up again. Am I the best barre student? No. But I love it and it reminds me I don't have to be perfect.*

True, there are times when perfectionistic tendencies pay off, and many of us would not be where we are today if we submitted sloppy, mediocre work. But keep perfectionism in check. Remember you do not have to meet 100% of the criteria to apply to the job, men will apply with only 60%, and they get the job. Instead of trying to reach perfection, work on progress over perfection. You will get a lot further, and often become a much nicer person to be around. Focus on progress and mastery of skills instead of attaining perfection. Which, as we have learned, is unattainable anyway.

PEOPLE-PLEASING

Self-limiting behavior #2? People-pleasing. People-pleasing is a convenient trap to avoid the possibility of failure. The thought process is that if everyone likes me, they won't let me fail. Rather than trust my abilities—i.e., confidence—it is safer to make people like me. But people-pleasing, like all of the self-limiting behaviors, doesn't work.

First off—you can't please everyone. Someone, somewhere, is bound to not like you. I'm going to go so far as to say, you don't even know what pleases other people. You think you are making them happy, but the reality is you can't read their mind. How do you know what they really want? And what makes one person happy may not make another person happy. As my mother used to say, "you can't please everyone." And yet we continue to try.

But here is the even more dangerous part of people-pleasing. When you work hard to please other people, you lose yourself. Ouch. I have been so into people-pleasing in the past, I totally lost myself. I had no idea what my favorite color was, or my favorite food, because it changed according to the people I was trying to please. I had no idea what I wanted because I was busy trying to please everyone else. Jane had totally disappeared.

Another problem with people-pleasing—on top of the fact that it doesn't work because you can't please everyone—is that it can lead to a dissolution of boundaries and eventual burnout. As a people-pleaser, if others come to you with a task, committee assignment, or additional work, you are likely to agree because you are more concerned with making them happy, than you are with setting boundaries for yourself and doing what you need. Saying "yes" may make others happy, but it can lead to stress and burnout for you.

What concerns me even more is that when I ask young women in particular to name the self-limiting behavior—perfectionism, people-pleasing, control, isolation, or busyness—that tends to trip them up the most, people-pleasing is currently the one most frequently cited. Why is people-pleasing so popular, especially among young women? My suspicion, confirmed by anectodal information, informal discussions, and observations, attributes the rise in people-pleasing to social media. No surprise. Everyone looks good on social media and everyone can measure how many people follow them, and yes, like them. A recipe for people-pleasing.

Here's the weird thing about people-pleasing. We think we know what people think about us. But do we really? No. Unless you're a mind reader—which most of us are not—we really have no idea if people like us, agree with us, etc. Furthermore, can you really control what people think about you? We'd like to think we can—by saying the right thing, agreeing with them, doing behaviors that please them—but the reality is that we cannot control what people think about us. Only they control what they think. So instead of focusing on what we can't control—other people's thoughts—a healthier perspective is to focus on what we CAN control—ourselves. One of my favorite quotations comes from Eleanor Roosevelt and was written long before social media had been invented: "No one can make you feel inferior without your consent." And I add, "Do not give them your consent!"

REFRAME PEOPLE-PLEASING

In a candid interview Awkwafina, the comedian, rapper, and actor from the hit movie, *Crazy Rich Asians*, and other films, admitted to being a people-pleaser. Who knew? I must admit I was taken aback and somewhat relieved to know that a woman as successful as Awkwafina struggles with people-pleasing like the rest of us. Instead of trying to please others, Awkwafina switched her thinking and focused on what she could control: her thoughts. Now, instead of trying to please others, she tries to treat everyone with respect and kindness. According to the actor, if she does that, she's done her job. Whether they like, approve, or support her, it is up to them and it is out of her control.

The second thing she does to minimize people-pleasing is avoiding social media. While eliminating it altogether may sound drastic, all things in moderation—even social media—may help reduce the propensity for people-pleasing. I've never seen an obituary that cited the number of likes the deceased received.

Practice

Identify the people who matter

In a one-inch square, write the names of people whose opinions matter to you. Hint: There shouldn't be many—hence on one inch. ☺ Who cares what the rest of the people think? Not you.

Be judicious with social media

As much as I would like to say to eliminate social media, I know that is unrealistic and a bit overboard. But moderation is the key. Identify social media sites that uplift and inspire you. Make a commitment to spend more time on positive sources and eliminate or limit the time spent on social media sites that do not make a positive contribution to your life. Use a timer for accountability.

Practice being kind and respectful to everyone
When the temptation is to say yes or decide to make someone else
happy (people-pleasing), make a conscious decision to instead,
treat them with respect and kindness. See the section on refusal
skills (how to say no politely) if you tend to take on additional
responsibility to avoid disappointing others.

Practice being kind and respectful to everyone
When the temptation is to say yes or decide to make someone else
happy (people-pleasing), make a conscious decision to instead,
treat them with respect and kindness. See the section on refusal
skills (how to say no politely) if you tend to take on additional
responsibility to avoid disappointing others.

SELF-LIMITING BEHAVIORS: CONTROL

As I have mentioned before, I have employed all these self-limiting behaviors at one time or another, but at this particular stage in my life, controlling behavior seems to be the one I struggle with the most. My false belief is that when I'm in charge and in control—frequently meaning I'm also doing all the work—is that everything gets done the way I want it done. The false assumption is that I will not fail. I'm doing the work and I'm doing it right. Wrong. Note the hint of perfectionism in this dysfunctional thinking. While I discuss the self-limiting behaviors as separate entities, the reality is that there is a lot of overlap between them.

There is a high price for being in control of everything and it's called burnout. You can't do everything. If you don't learn to delegate tasks, you are on the road to a slow sizzle. A recent survey found that while percentages vary among industries, almost 50% of the entry level workforce is comprised of women. Hence, a relatively equal number of men and women start careers. Yet as you progress up the corporate ladder, that gender balance starts to become skewed. Recent stats show that only 10% of CEOs are female. While this number is an improvement, it still lags behind the 90% of all CEOs who are male. There are many reasons for the lack of women in top leadership positions, but if we don't learn to delegate household tasks, childcare tasks, and job tasks, we are likely to be exhausted, sick, and burned out. No wonder we lack the stamina to make it to the top.

Learning to delegate is easier said than done. I was fortunate to have a woman friend whose superpower was delegating, and I learned from her. When necessary, she took time to teach the other person how to do the job. She communicated clear expectations, such as regular check in times and ownership over assignments. But the hardest thing about delegating for me is that it requires me to be comfortable with someone doing things differently than the way I would. Ouch. I have had to learn there are other ways, besides my way, that work.

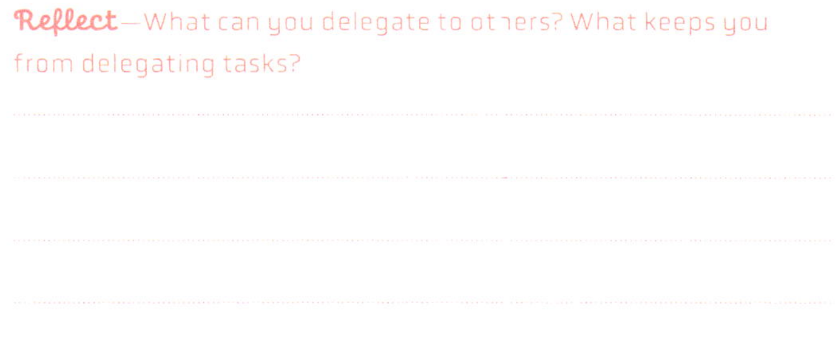

The only way to learn to delegate is to practice and start small. Full disclosure—letting go is hard and scary. While teaching a full load and grading over 2,500 resilience papers in one semester, it became obvious that I needed help and needed to earn to delegate this task to the teaching assistants. I was, of course, convinced that no one grades better than I do which is an embarrassing example of my inflated ego. Still skeptical that I could trust this important task to others (implied—less qualified than me), I cautiously relinquished the grading of student resilience papers to teaching assistants. Once again, my over-inflated ego reared its ugly head. Imagine my surprise, and relief, when I realized the women were learning resilience regardless of who did the grading. The papers weren't graded exactly the way I would have graded them. I wish the teaching assistants made more comments, and I wish they required more elaboration in the response. But it worked. The young women still learned resilience and I could spend my time doing other things, once I learned to delegate this task to someone else.

Likewise, when overwhelmed with child-rearing, work, and managing the household, I learned to delegate grocery shopping to my husband.

Side note. *In the early history of humankind men were the hunters. They would leave the cave, hunt for food, and bring back their catch for the woman to prepare. I like to think that delegating grocery shopping helps satisfy my husband's primeval instinct for hunting. Hehe.*

Notice I used the word "learned" when I talk about delegating. Does he do grocery shopping the way I would? No. Buy exactly the things I would buy? No. Is his grocery shopping perfect? No. And sometimes, I confess, I lament to myself about how I do it better. But do I really want to pay the physical, psychological, and emotional price to control everything? The answer is no. Delegating to others is good enough, and that frees me up to do other things.

> **Practice**—There's only one way I know how to learn to delegate and that is practice. Think of a small task you can delegate to someone. Something that will not matter if it is not done perfectly. Do it!

> *When delegating, what will you do to help them succeed? For example, I meet with my teaching assistants to review the grading criteria, so they are confident they are grading appropriately. I give my husband a grocery list—sometimes complete with picture of the products—to help him get the right items*

REFRAME CONTROL

The way I like to reframe letting go of control (can you tell how much I struggle with this), is that by delegating a task to others, I allow them to learn a new skill and to shine in their accomplishments. That's right. I've learned to think of delegating as opening opportunities for others to excel and that makes me happy. Thinking positively about delegating and using it to promote others while I step into the background, makes letting go a little easier. And honestly, I have yet to regret delegating tasks. My goal is to keep practicing. I wonder how much burnout, exhaustion, illness, and feelings of being overwhelmed, could be eliminated or at least, reduced, if we were better at letting go of control and delegating more.

Is letting go easy? No way. I must constantly practice and remind myself I'm creating opportunities for others and taking care of myself. A colleague and I are currently in the midst of developing a leadership institute. We are trying to practice delegating. Instead of both of us attending events, one of us will go to the event which frees the other to do something else. Is it hard? Yes. We are both go-getters and doers. But we frequently remind each other that only one of us needs to make an appearance and the freedom of delegating keeps us both motivated, enthusiastic, and mentally healthy.

Reflect—What did you delegate? How did it go? Was it hard? Did it give you a break? Did you learn to accept that it is not done exactly how you would do it? How did that feel? What did you have time to do as a result of delegating a task to someone else? I hope it was fun and rewarding.

ISOLATION

The frustrating thing about self-limiting behaviors is that there are enough people who want to limit us in the first place— we should not be limiting ourselves with dysfunctional behavior. Isolation is another way we try to avoid the possibility of failure. Spoiler alert: it doesn't work.

What do I mean by isolation? I have, unfortunately, isolated myself in certain job situations as a survival mechanism. Scared that a colleague, boss, or subordinate might discover that I don't have all the answers, that I don't know what to do, or that I'm not perfect (note how perfectionism seems to keep creeping in), I isolate myself and pretend I know what I'm doing. I try to "fake it 'till I make it," but I'm not good at faking and I'm scared to death I'm not going to make it. I'm afraid to ask for help because I might appear weak or unqualified, so I struggle to do everything alone. Similar to the imposter syndrome, rather than ask for help, I live my career in terror that people will discover I'm not as smart/good as everyone thinks I am, and if they get close to me, they will discover I'm a fake. In other words, if you truly knew me, you wouldn't like me. The way I can continue this façade of having my act together when I don't, is to not get close to people, isolate myself, and pretend to appear competent by not needing help from anyone. Or in the words of Brené Brown, I "armor up," pretend I'm tough, and make it look like I can do it by myself, a.k.a. the rugged individualist.

There is a real downside to isolation. First off, we were never created to work in isolation; we were made for community. It is not an accident that one of the most brutal forms of punishment is solitary confinement. Isolation is deadly to the mind, body, and spirit, as we learned only too well during the COVID-19 pandemic while we sheltered in place.

But there's another issue at play, when we isolate ourselves, we pretend we've got this and are in control. And that may not be true, but we have no feedback to tell us otherwise. This can be limiting to our productivity and creativity (Yikes—once again these self-limiting behaviors tend to blur together). It takes a lot of energy to be something you're not. When we armor up and pretend to be tough and independent, we take our energy—which is a limited resource—and instead of using it to solve a problem or think creatively, we use it to protect ourselves. When a dear friend and colleague of mine came out as gay, his creativity, problem-solving skills, and career soared like never before. I wonder how much of his energy in the past had been spent on maintaining the status quo. Once he wasn't trying to be someone he wasn't, he could use his energy in far more productive and creative ways.

In the early stages of my career, as a young college grad, I found myself in the manufacturing (predominately male) division of a company in the HVAC—heating, ventilation, air conditioning—(predominately male) industry. That's right. I was a manager in the manufacturing division of a company that sold furnaces and air conditioners. In fact, the company at that time was so predominately male, that I was the sole woman manager in my corporate division—which was not all that unusual given the time period and industry. There were no women role models, no women mentors, and virtually no women higher ranking than me from whom I could learn or emulate. I was isolated through no fault of my own. However, in my efforts to fit in with the other managers (a.k.a. men) I attempted to pretend I was tough, heartless, and could be just as tough as a man if that's what it took to advance my career. That didn't last long. I'm not heartless; in fact, I care deeply about people. And I'm not tough; I am sensitive and can be easily wounded by mean words. I used my energy to isolate myself and pretend I knew what I was doing. And after a few years, exhausted from trying to be something I'm not, I quit.

Instead of being tough, the way I like to visualize strength now is like a strong backbone and a soft heart. My strong backbone keeps me upright and allows me to bounce back after setbacks or failures. My soft heart allows me to care. One of my favorite quotations comes from Chloé Zhao, an Asian-American film director and Academy Award winner. She sees her challenge as trying to "stay soft in an industry that wants to take that power away." I like to think of it as having a strong backbone and a kind heart. Isolation makes it appear that we are in control, perfect, and know what we're doing. But in reality, we are only pretending and isolating ourselves from good people. Staying soft is powerful.

Another way I fight isolation is by finding someone to mentor. I know, it sounds strange to ask you to find someone to mentor when the traditional mentor format is usually reversed; people ask you to mentor them. I've served as a mentor and mentee in a variety of instances—both formal and informal—and the relationship has worked OK. But the mentor/mentee relationships that stick in my mind as impactful are the ones when I subtly selected a bright, energetic, and enthusiastic student or new colleague to mentor. You don't have to call it mentoring—I never did. I invited my chosen mentee for coffee, lunch, phone call, or walk. We hit it off, found lots to talk about and problems to solve, and in each case, kept meeting regularly for anywhere from a semester to years. In all cases, we still stay in touch. Supposedly the mentee is the one who reaps the most rewards from the relationship, but it seems to me, I'm the one who really benefits. Helping someone always makes me feel better and I am continually shocked at how a little comment can have a big impact. It seems to me like I'm hardly helping at all—doesn't everyone know this? And yet, no, not everyone knows what seems obvious to me. Helping a younger colleague or student reminds me that I know more than I give myself credit for. Sharing my experiences and well-earned knowledge helps other people. Helping someone else helps us realize we are not alone and builds life-long relationships. Choosing someone to mentor is one of my favorite ways to avoid isolation.

BUSYNESS

Ironically, this section almost got left out of the book. Why? Because I'm too busy to write it. Sound familiar? I have a manuscript deadline and the work keeps getting piled on. And yet, in my heart of hearts, I knew I needed to write at least a few words about busyness and how it can be used as an avoidance strategy that I know only too well. Note that I didn't call this section success, or productivity, or results—it's busyness. We keep ourselves busy to avoid things we don't want to think about or deal with. Business also helps us project the image that we're successful and sought after. After all, why else would we be so busy?

What's the problem with busyness and why is the behavior self-limiting? First off, it's exhausting. Just like control, it is exhausting to be busy all the time. Of course, there are always external factors in play. Some careers have built in busy times that eventually give way to a much-needed breaks or at least a slow-down in work. For example, I hate to bother my friend who is a CPA until a couple of weeks after April 15 and things are starting to calm down at the office. Another friend who pastors a church breathes a sigh of relief once the fun but busy festivities of the Christmas season are over. Cruise ship employees work weeks on board almost non-stop but then receive an uninterrupted break on shore before the next cruise. Yet many professions, such as motherhood, don't have that luxury. It was a rude awakening when I realized that to my newborn, a weekend was just another day and there was no break for mom. I can't help by think that with all the busyness and frenetic activity, we will wear ourselves out and burn out before we achieve our dreams.

It's like running. I used to run for fun and exercise. And let's be honest here—I call what I do, running; the women athletes I mentor, who are Division 1 NCAA competitive track team members, would politely call what I do jogging on a fast day, and fast walking on a typical day. But nonetheless, I would lace up my Nikes, hit the pavement, and call myself a runner. The only way I made it to the end of a run or race was by pacing myself. If I went full out at the beginning, I had no energy left to finish. The same holds true for busyness. Unless you're planning on dying young, life is a marathon, not a sprint. Busyness wears us out before we can make it to the finish line.

A second problem with busyness is how distracting it is. One of the wisest women I know would constantly chide me about going down rabbit holes when I would tell her all the projects I was working on. She was wise enough to see through my façade. By getting sucked into a myriad of projects—all of which were good, but time consuming, and not my calling—I stayed busy and unproductive. All that busyness accomplished was to distract me from my North Star—my true calling and what I should be working on. Why did I let these busy distractors in my life? Because sometimes pursuing a passion or calling is hard. It is painful and it hurts, but you know that's where you're supposed to be. And busyness gives you a temporary escape.

Finally, busyness can make you sick. Literally sick. We were not designed to work 24/7. We were designed to rest. In fact, it's one of the Ten Commandments. Like "fear not" we haven't gotten that message either. Yet I did not model rest well for my daughters and I suspect I'm not the only mom who failed at that one. Back in the day, the only time I would rest is when I got sick. That's right. I would push myself so relentlessly that my body would finally give up and I would find myself flat on my back in bed. Sick. The really sad thing was that I was glad to be sick so I could get a rest. And according to a recent article, I am not alone in this. Other mothers also daydream about being hospitalized. Don't get me wrong—we may love what we do and love our families. But busyness is exhausting. After way too many years of pushing myself to illness, I finally decided enough. I am learning to rest, letting go of the busyness and coaching other women to do the same.

The really dangerous thing about keeping busy all the time is that it is a socially acceptable approach to denial. We tend to respect, admire, even idolize people who seem to be busy all the time. We hesitate to approach them because "she's so busy" (which is another reason why I am easily seduced by busyness) and they are able to remain isolated—feeding into another self-limiting behavior. I must admit, I continually struggle with this self-limiting behavior and probably always will. Why? Because the high-achieving people I hang around are all busy. Granted, none would have achieved greatness without a lot of hard work. But hard work taken to the extreme becomes busyness, and I'm surrounded by it all the time.

When I find myself lapsing into busyness and feeling nervous that I might have a block of time with nothing scheduled (oh no—I will have to intentionally think about what I'm doing instead of blindly staying busy) I remind myself of my focus. It took me a while to declare—to myself and to the world—what issues were important to me, but once I made that determination, managing my time and focus were simpli-fied. While I should have known a long time ago that my passion was empowering women, it took me a long time, a lot of rabbit holes, and way too many years where I spread myself way too thin, before I realized the value of focus. Now, when faced with decisions about getting involved, I ask myself, is it related to serving God or empowering women? If the answer is no, I decline. The result is that I am happier, healthier, and able to make a bigger impact in the selected areas I have chosen.

> **Practice**—*Think of three issues that are important to you. If you have a hard time narrowing it to three, start by listing them all. Give a score to how you feel about each one. My guess is that with careful accounting, your three most important passions will eventually rise to the top. Use these as your North Star guiding light to point you in the direction you should go.*

Meanwhile, I got to run. I would like to write more, but no time. Multiple deadlines are looming. And yes, I've still not mastered letting go of busyness.

WHY ARE WE SO AFRAID OF FAILURE?

LET'S TALK ABOUT THE F-WORD: FAILURE

We've talked about self-limiting behaviors and how they hold us back. Underlying those self-defeating behaviors is our fear of failure: the ultimate predator that causes us to limit ourselves. There are enough people out there who want to limit us. We do not need to limit ourselves.

WHAT DO I MEAN BY FAILURE?

When I use the word failure throughout this guided journal, I'm using it as a broad umbrella term. If failure sounds too harsh, think of it as a mistake, or misstep, or roadblock—something that didn't turn out as you had planned.

I like to think of failure as a continuum. On the right side are big failures. I lost my job. I lost my marriage. I lost my bank account. I lost my house. These are BIG failures that hopefully you will rarely experience throughout the course of your life. However, I'm old enough to have experienced a few. And I can state from first-hand experience, the same resilience strategies that help me recover from small mistakes also helped me deal with larger losses.

At the other side of the continuum, are small failures. Here are some of my personal examples. I slept through my alarm and missed a meeting. I shouldn't have said something in a meeting (happens all the time). Darn. Or, equally as frustrating, I wish I would have said something in a meeting. Drat. I should have put him in his place and I missed my chance. I was going to run 5 miles today, but only ran 2. Or my personal favorite—I was going to eat only two Girl Scout Thin Mints cookies and instead, I ate the entire roll. (Seriously. How can you stop eating Thin Mints once you've opened the roll???). This—the small failures, mistakes, shortcomings, mishaps, or speedbumps—is where we practice building resilience, learning confidence, and getting past our fear of failure.

Like anything, you don't practice interview questions during an interview for your dream job; you practice with friends and in less important job interviews. That way, when your dream opportunity arises, you've practiced and you're prepared. We'll do the same here. We're going to practice building resilience by reframing smaller failures—didn't get the job, said something stupid, messed up an order while waitressing, or got a B+ instead of an A. You don't practice your free throws when the state championship is on the line. You practice free throws in your driveway so that when the state championship is on the line, you know what to do. While we will practice building resilience with smaller failures, know that these same skills can be used to reframe larger failures. I know from experience.

As part of sales, I coach women to become resilient because rejection is inevitable. Without resilience, failure could be the end of an otherwise lucrative and promising career. To reinforce resilience as a default strategy and not a one-off that disappears once the coach disappears, I encourage women to journal about their failures and how they practiced resilience—not just once, but at least five times over the course of a couple of months. In many cases, the women share their writings with me and I respond. To date, I've read over 2,500 journal entries about failure and resilience. And guess what I learned about failure? My observation is that 95–98% of the failures listed in the women's journal entries were self-imposed. That is, they were the ones deciding that they had failed—it was not a supervisor, friend, co-worker, or family member who told them they missed the mark. Occasionally a supervisor or manager was disappointed with the writer's performance. But in the vast majority of cases, the event was classified as a failure because the woman did not meet her own high—dare I say unrealistic—expectations of herself. In the majority of cases, it's not the world telling us we've failed, it's us telling us we've failed. Ouch!

FEAR OF FAILURE

But it's not the failure itself that concerns me. We all eventually learn that one mediocre job review is not the end of the world. It's not the failure itself—a mistake can be fixed. What I'm concerned about is the *fear* of failure—not taking action because you're afraid you *might* fail, not because you have failed. You avoid taking a risk which is the flip side of an opportunity, because of the fear that you might fail.

Fear is deadly. We can overcome failure—in fact, we learn from our mistakes. But if we are afraid to fail and never take a risk, we deprive ourselves from the learning. Fear masquerades by various names. I like to call it fear, but others call it anxiety, worry, or insecurity. Even Imposter Syndrome is rooted in fear—the fear that someone might find out that I'm not perfect or that I don't have all the answers. Biblical scholars claim that "fear not" is the most repeated verse in the Bible; clearly we haven't gotten the message yet.

RESILIENCE IS THE ANTIDOTE TO FEAR OF FAILURE

Before we go any further, I want to make it clear what we're talking about. The term resilience gets a lot of press these days. As a former English major taught to value the accuracy of word choice, it drives me nuts because in many (most?) cases the word "resilience" is misused and frequently interchanged with persistence, which it is not. I go crazy when someone uses the word "resilience" when what they really mean is persistence—a related, but different term. For the sake of my sanity and communication clarity, let's make these definitions clear. For the purposes of this text, I define resilience as *the ability to bounce back quickly after failure.*

When I think of resilience, I think of those blow up, punching bag clowns with a weighted base that were kids' toys. The point of the toy was that you would punch the clown, (in retrospect, that seems a bit violent—but this was way before video games) and the clown would bounce right back in position, as if it had never been hit. That's resilience. It's the ability to bounce back quickly after failure. Instead of ruminating, reacting, and refraining, all of which is time consuming, emotionally draining, and self-defeating, resilience enables the individual to move on quickly after a failure.

Successful entrepreneurs have a saying: fail fast. What does that mean? It means that if you are an entrepreneur, you are likely to fail and fail more than once. If you take time to ruminate, react, and refrain, you will never get to work on your next big idea. Entrepreneurs with resilience get over their failure quickly and get on to their next big invention.

RESILIENCE IS NOT PERSISTENCE

Resilience is distinct from persistence, which means to keep going in spite of adversity. For example, when my barre3 instructor coaxes us into holding a physically challenging plank pose (like a push up without movement) for way too long, she reminds us we are "resilient." If I wasn't too exhausted trying to hold the plank, I'd yell "No! No! No!—we are not resilient in holding this pose! The word is persistent! Persistent! Not resilient!" Lucky for her, I'm too exhausted trying to keep with the class to protest her misuse of language. But it clearly upsets me.

Nothing is wrong with persistence. It is an admirable trait in some circumstances. But sticking it out no matter what—persistence—is very different from resilience. Persistence would tell you to keep running a marathon even though you have a broken leg, because you need to press on no matter what. Resilience is when you are flat on the ground mired in failure, feeling defeated and discouraged, yet you pick yourself up and continue on and try again or try something new. You do not stay stuck. Resilience means that you have hit rock bottom and yet, have the resilience to pull yourself back up. Persistence does not allow for the hitting of rock bottom—a.k.a., failure.

To reiterate, persistence has its value but that is not what we are talking about here. And later on, you'll see how, in some cases, to be resilient you have to quit (i.e. not persist and remove yourself from a toxic situation) to succeed. More on that in the section on resilience strategies. But for now, remember that resilience is different from per-sistence—in spite of what the general public might say.

WHAT IS CONFIDENCE?

So how does all of this relate to confidence? I define confidence as belief in your abilities. Simple as that. I can do this. I can finish this race. I can speak up in this meeting. I can ask for the sale. I can run for election. I can serve as a leader.

Note what confidence is not. Confidence doesn't say you have to win, be the best, or be perfect. You may not win the race. Not everyone will like your idea when you speak up in the meeting. You may not get the sale. You may not win the election. Confidence doesn't comment on the outcome—confidence is the ability to do the task. Period. Do the work. Let go of the outcome.

There is no comparison in confidence. Once again, I'm confident I can perform the task. I'm not saying I can do it better than you or worse than you. I'm saying I can do the task. Keep the blinders on and focus on what you can do—run the race, speak up, take a risk. I'm fond of adding a postscript to the quotation "Comparison robs you of joy." Comparison also robs you of confidence because there will always be someone worse off than you and, rest assured, there will always be someone better. No comparisons.

How do you learn confidence? You learn confidence from practice. For example, I am confident of my ability to mentor young women as they start their careers. How did I get that confidence? The ability to coach may be one of my gifts but I also diligently practice my craft. I experiment with different techniques and tools and I cultivate the ones that work and eliminate the ones that fail. As a result of over 30 years of experience working with young women, I am confident in my ability as a mentor.

How did my daughter learn to have confidence in her ability to make free throws when she played basketball? Because, being the good Hoosier that I am, I made her practice 100 free throws every day (I shagged the balls and counted) in our driveway. I even recruited our border collie to bark and whine as a distraction to simulate an antagonistic crowd. When Joan went to the free throw line, she was confident that the ball would go in the basket. And I was too. Did she make every free throw? Of course not. But she made more than she missed and because she practiced, she walked to the free throw line with confidence. Just call me coach.

AND NO, IT'S NOT SELF-CONFIDENCE; IT'S CONFIDENCE

While we're at it, let's talk about another misused term: self-confidence. I'm not a fan of the term self-confidence. Not saying it's right or wrong, but the global concept that someone is self-confident does not track with my experience, observation, or research. I conceive of confidence as being contextually bound. What I mean by contextually bound is that you can be confident of your abilities in some areas of your life and less confident of your abilities in other arenas.

My level of confidence in my ability to plan an event—whether that be a workshop for professional women, a wedding, or Thanksgiving dinner—is practically non-existent. Planning an event is my worst nightmare. What if no one comes? What do you serve? How are you going to invite people? What are you going to talk about? And my list of fears goes on and on. As I write this, I am in the event planning process for a Women Talking event: a gathering of professional women and college women where they share their frustrations and advice when engaging in predominately male professions. My stomach is in knots thinking about the event and I have expressed that fear to everyone and anyone who will listen.

But this I do know. By following the same process used to hone my consulting skills—practice, evaluate, tweak, and practice again—I can learn to have confidence in my ability to plan and host events. The secret sauce is in finding or creating opportunities to practice, which might involve making mistakes with low consequences. For example, this is the second time I've been involved with the production of the Women Talking event. I helped plan the initial event, so I have an idea of what to do. This is the first time I'm leading the event. While I eventually plan to expand the event to a larger audience and increase the cost to participants, for the second event, I'm holding the attendance to a number slightly above the initial event and charging a minimal amount ($30 per person) which is more than the first event which was free, and is less than what I plan on charging in subsequent events when the event is established. Baby steps. I may never quit my day job to become an event planner—I truly don't think the gift of hospitality is in my bones—but I can become confident in my ability to pull off an event if I need to. Confidence is a learned skill. And if I can learn it, you can too. And once you learn confidence in one area of your life, you can take that same process and adapt it to another area as needed. And PS: the Women Talking event was a huge success.

WHAT HAPPENS WHEN WE FAIL? THE FAILURE PROCESS

OK. So, some of you might think I'm carrying this fear of failure piece a little too far by mapping out the failure process. But I think it's important that we identify exactly why we're so afraid of failing. And the failure process plays an important part in our fears. As the daughter of an engineer, while other dads were taking their kids to Disneyland for vacation, my father was dragging us through factory tours. I'm serious. I've seen how Ford automobiles were made, how Kellogg's Corn Flakes are processed, how Sap's donuts are baked and even how Kodak cameras are produced. And the list goes on. I didn't always appreciate the factory tours as a youngster. OK, I didn't like them at all and I couldn't understand why we didn't go to Disneyland like the other kids. But as an adult, I've come to appreciate the factory tours, and my father's engineering background gave me appreciate for process design. Little wonder as a doctoral student, I studied the consumer behavior decision process and the sales process. Likewise, we need to look at the steps in the failure process.

FAILING HURTS

To add insult to injury, besides all the things that people think or say about us if we fail, there are also not-so-good thoughts rattling around our heads when we fail that cause additional pain. And let's be honest. I'm into comfort and will avoid pain any chance I get. So rather than deal with the possibility of failure, I avoid risk and limit myself and I bet you do the same (see the section on self-limiting behaviors). For now, I want you to think about what happens in your head when you fail or make a mistake. I call these steps "the three R's." No—not reading, writing and arithmetic. When we fail, we tend to ruminate, reprove, and refrain and believe me, that's no fun. No wonder we avoid the possibility of failure at all costs. And avoiding risk, and the opportunities it presents, costs us a lot.

RUMINATE—WE KEEP REPLAYING THE MISTAKE IN OUR HEADS

Think about what happens when you fail. If you're like me and other women, you tend to ruminate about your failure. To be clear, ruination in moderation is not bad. Reflecting upon mistakes holds us accountable and helps prevent similar mistakes in the future. Learning from mistakes is good but that's not what I'm talking about here. I'm talking about playing and replaying the mistake over and over and over again in your head. It's like an ESPN film clip playing in a continuous loop. Some poor kid misses a field goal, costs the team the game, and ruins everyone's life. And thanks to the marvel of film, that mistake gets played on national TV, Instagram, and TikTok over, and over, and over again.

A similar thing happens when we fail. We play our mistake over, and over, again in our heads. Why? It makes no sense. Do I think the ending will be different if I keep rehashing the incident? As we all know, the ending doesn't change. And in fact, by replaying the incident in our head, we are reinforcing the mistake and encrypting it into our memory. Great.

Remember how you memorized your phone number when you were in kindergarten? You repeated it over and over until it was etched in your memory—never to be forgotten. Replaying our failures over and over again in our heads has the same effect. Instead of forgetting the incident and moving on, we stay stuck in our error. No wonder we don't want to take a chance on failing—who wants to keep reviewing the mistake over, and over again, in their head?

To make matters worse, research suggests that women ruminate more than men. From personal experience as well as observation, I believe it. However, I have to say from my experiences interacting with male colleagues and mentoring them as well, I believe men ruminate too. My guess is that men are less likely to admit that they ruminate; hence the discrepancy with the data and my observations.

REPROVE—WE BEAT OURSELVES UP

In addition to replaying the failure over, and over, again in our heads, we also beat ourselves up—or reprove ourselves—for making a mistake. While replaying the failure, I'm mentally trash-talking myself—what a stupid mistake, how could I have made such a stupid mistake, now everyone thinks I am stupid because of my stupid mistake and the mental beating goes on and on. Why? Why do we think that beating ourselves up and punishing ourselves will stop the behavior? When you mentally beat yourself up, all you get is pain, not improvement.

So why do we keep doing it? I suspect we think that by mentally beating ourselves up, we will not engage in the behavior again—like getting spanked as a little kid. But we're not little kids anymore and a beating—mentally or physically—hurts. I'm not going to risk the chance of failing if getting beat up is a likely outcome.

When mentally beating myself up (don't forget, I am the Queen of Failure) I tend to head to dark places and make assumptions about what other people are thinking about me. As we discussed in the people-pleasing section, we don't really know what people are thinking. We think we do but, unless you're a mind reader or God—and neither of which is likely—we don't actually know what other people are thinking. We think they don't like us, or are laughing at us, or are calling us idiots behind our backs. But the reality is, we don't actually know that. As I remind other women and myself, I have no idea what others are thinking. I'm not a mind reader, and more than likely, neither are you. So maybe it's time to stop the mental abuse.

One of the most dangerous misperceptions is that we think everyone is paying attention to us. Thinking that all eyes are on us and that everyone remembers exactly what we said, wore, etc. is debilitating. Unless you are Taylor Swift—or someone of similar fame—the reality is that people are not likely as focused on you as you think they are. What are people truly focused on? Their favorite topic—themselves. Don't believe me? Try this little exercise with a friend. I love watching students do it when I assign it in class and I love practicing it. It is hard. Especially for those of us—I'm looking at you—who are like me and who, in conversation, are not really listening to you but instead are focusing on the next brilliant statement I'm going to make. Sound familiar?

Why is this so hard? It's hard because we stop listening about halfway through a sentence so that we can create some brilliant response. I use this exercise to demonstrate that people are not paying attention to you—they're paying attention to themselves and their brilliant responses. Next time you find yourself becoming self-conscious and feel like everyone is looking at you remind yourself that what they are really thinking about is themselves.

REFRAIN—WE DECIDE WE'RE NEVER DOING THAT AGAIN

To review, when we fail, we **ruminate**, we beat ourselves up—**reprove**—then we **refrain**. We tell ourselves, "I'm never doing that again." Ouch. The first two reactions to failure are painful, but the last reaction—refraining from ever doing that again—is deadly. If you quit after one failure, you're stuck. You'll never go anywhere. A recent *Harvard Business Review* article reported that women are 40% less likely than men to reapply for a leadership position after being turned down. Whoa! Think about that for a minute. Instead of learning from the initial application and applying again, women tend to stop applying. And the problem with that is that you will never get anywhere if you don't apply. I would maintain that few of us succeed on our first try and that success comes after multiple attempts. If you quit after the first try, you'll never get anywhere.

I could overwhelm you with examples where I have tried once, failed, and refused to try again, but one of the most vivid examples, and when I started practicing what I was teaching, came in the form of a teaching award. I pride myself on being a good professor, so imagine my dismay when I did not get the teaching award for which I had so judiciously applied. To add insult to injury, a person I could not stand,

and, in my not-so-humble-opinion was not as good of a teacher as I was, won the award. I was furious and stormed into my department head's office whining and complaining about how the award winner was underserving and how I had been cheated. To her credit, she patiently listened to my whining (could I please have a little cheese to go with my whine?), then reminded me of my own words. If you don't apply, you will never get it. She basically told me to shut up, get back to my office, and work on next year's application. I did. And didn't win. So, I applied a third time. And you are reading the words of an award-winning university professor.

IF YOU'RE NOT FAILING, YOU'RE NOT TRYING

Why is fear of failure so paralyzing? Because if you are afraid of failing, you will never take a risk, try something new, and get outside your comfort zone. Fear of failure keeps us trapped inside our supposedly comfortable cocoons which are, in reality, suffocating our potential. And stuck we stay. To become butterflies, we have to a take risk and crack out of the cocoon.

The connection between fear of failure and taking a risk—whether it be signing up for a course outside your major, applying for a new position, moving to a new location, or just doing something different— was vividly illustrated by a former young man I was mentoring. As part of learning how to sell, future salespeople have to practice failing (more on that later) so that they will be able to move on quickly from rejection in the sales world. When discussing failure and subsequent resilience, one young man commented that he was unable to contribute to the discussion because he hadn't failed at anything that week. Seriously?!? I raised an eyebrow and probably gave him a skeptical look. Later, he wrote me an insightful email. He realized the reason he hadn't failed, and consequently had been unable to contribute to the discussion, was that he never tried anything new. He keeps within his comfort zone where he is assured of success and thus avoids any possibility of failure. Eureka. And I'm not talking about the vacuum cleaner company. The lightbulb went on for him, and me, and he has since learned how to tiptoe outside his comfort zone to much success. I will always be grateful to him for sharing his insight with me and we have stayed in touch over the years.

R2 = C THE CONNECTION BETWEEN RISK (FEAR OF FAILURE), RESILIENCE, AND CONFIDENCE

The antidote to fear of failure is not making friends with failure (seriously?!?) or welcoming failure (are you kidding me—you might as well welcome Jack the Ripper). Learning from failure is helpful, but beware because taken to the extreme, it can lead to excessive rumination. The key to overcoming fear of failure is practicing resilience. Note that I didn't say eliminating your fear of failure. Fear will always be there. I feel it every time I parallel park my car, take on a new consulting client, or wonder if the module I recorded last year will be embraced by clients this year as well. The fear of trying something new—taking a risk—will always be there. But if you have learned to practice resilience, the fear is not paralyzing. Prior to delivering my TEDx talk—one of the most terrifying things I have ever done because it is saved for posterity and broadcast over the unlimited internet—a colleague reminded me that the definition of courage is "feeling the fear and moving forward anyway." I like that. You will never eliminate the fear that you might fail when you take a risk, but if you are resilient and you know you can bounce back from failure, the fear no longer paralyzes you from trying something new.

Resilience and confidence work together in helping us reclaim our strength, power, and voice and play a crucial role in getting past our fear of failure. If you're afraid of failing, you won't take a risk—apply for a stretch job, run for office, speak up in a meeting where you're the only woman—because you might fail. Game over. You may have enough courage to take the risk and speak up, but if you get shut down (more on that in the communication section), and you lack resilience, you'll be afraid to speak up again. You tried, you failed, and without resilience, you'll never try again. But if you are resilient, you're more likely to take a risk—what's the worst that could happen?—and if it doesn't go exactly perfect the first time—likely because it's the first time—you'll try again because you are able to bounce back quickly after failure. And the fact that you're willing to try again, and again, and even again, puts you on the road to becoming confident because you've practiced doing it so many times. Resilience cultivates confidence. Resilience neutralizes our fear of failure and gives us the courage to take a risk.

In fact, in my use of this exercise in multiple settings, I've never lost a person yet. I will admit, when talking with a group of lawyers, a couple of people did, in fact, get $20. I'm not sure how to explain that except that maybe lawyers make more money than the rest of us, but I digress. The point of this exercise is to illustrate resilience. You didn't get what you wanted and yet you didn't die. What's the worst that can happen? They say no. And no one dies. This is the mindset we will learn to adopt when we start practicing resilience strategies. More to come.

RESILIENCE STRATEGIES

We've been talking about how we limit ourselves to placate our fear of failure. Ready for some good news? Resilience is the key to cultivating confidence and both resilience and confidence are learned skills. I learned them. The young women I mentor learned them. And you can learn them. This section is entitled resilience strategies—not tactics, not beliefs, not behaviors—strategies. Why? I like the word strategy and women have long had to learn to be strategic. We've never had the luxury of physical power or social power, so we've always had to look for strategic openings to make our move. So here are the strategies and here we come!

DISCIPLINE YOUR THOUGHTS

- Press pause and change the tape
- Know when to quit

REFRAMING PAST REGRETS

- Failure is an event, not a person
- Seeing failure as courage

FIND YOUR ALLIES

- Set a timer on the pity party
- Confide in a friend

TIME PERSPECTIVE

- Think positive in the process
- Be patient

The strategies are categorized into four quadrants to make them easier to remember. Moving clockwise from left to right, the first quadrant is labeled **Discipline Your Thoughts**. This is because, you guessed it, these strategies require discipline. I have to work on "Press pause and change the tape" almost daily and just when I think I have mastered it, some ugly tape recording starts playing in my head again. "Know when to quit" is a strategy to be used judiciously. I don't use it often, and I'm always scared when I do, but sometimes quitting is the smartest road to resilience and bouncing back.

To the right of Discipline Your Thoughts lies **Reframing Past Regrets**. These are two of my personal favorite strategies and are among the ones that I use the most. When we reframe a situation, we think about it from a different perspective and that's exactly what these strategies do. "Failure is an event, not a person" places the emphasis where it belongs—on the event, not your identity. And "Seeing failure as courage" requires you to be proud that you took a risk—regardless of the outcome.

Time Perspective sits below Reframing Past Regrets. "Think positive in the process," as the name suggests, involves not succumbing to downward spiraling thoughts when in the midst of the situation. And "Be patient," one of the strategies I dislike the most but have learned to employ, suggests that sometimes the failure had nothing to do with you. Patience is required to wait for the next opportunity. Yuck.

Finally, in the **Find Your Allies** category are strategies relating to others. A personal favorite as a mother, a leader, and a favorite of young women I mentor is "Set a timer on the pity party." Before being crowned the Queen of Failure, I was the Princess of Pity Parties. No one threw a better pity party than me. Working with allies helped me minimize the time spent wallowing in my self-pity. "Confide in a friend" involves sharing your fears and becoming vulnerable with someone you trust. An effective strategy but easier said than done.

As we peruse these different strategies, think of this as a shopping trip. Full disclosure. Like my attitude toward cooking, I really don't like shopping either. Yes: I know. I've spent untold hours studying and teaching consumer behavior. I appreciate the steps in the consumer decision process. But I hate to shop. Regardless, like my attitude toward cooking, I can do it when necessary. The point is, if we were shopping, we'd all like different outfits. What looks good on me may not look good on you. What looks great on the hanger, may look horrible when I try it on. What I would choose for a wedding would be different from what I would choose for a workout. The point is, you need to try these strategies and determine how they work for you. I have my favorite go-to strategies and the women I mentor have theirs. I encourage you to try them all and see which ones you like.

—As we learn about resilience, start practicing these strategies by keeping a resilience journal. Here's what I do and what I coach other women to do.

1. First, identify the failure. Bonus points if you recognize the source of the failure. Did someone tell you that you failed? For example, you messed up their order while waiting tables? Or did you let yourself down? My bet is that you are the one who determined you failed. Start giving yourself some grace.

2. Second, apply one of these resilience strategies. In the messed-up food order, for example, maybe you use "Failure is an event, not a person."

3. Then reflect. Did the strategy allow you to forgive yourself for making a mistake and get over the failure quickly? Or are you still beating yourself up? If you're still beating yourself up, try a different strategy. But if it allowed you to move on and quit wallowing in guilt, you may be on your way to becoming more resilient.

When I first started experimenting with this technique as a way to build resilience, I wasn't sure how many times we needed to practice failing so we could practice resilience. The women I mentored wrote about practicing failing, applying a resilience strategy, and reflecting if the strategy helped them rebound from the failure quickly. The first time I experimented with this method, eight practice rounds were suggested as the minimum number of practices required before resilience would replace resignation as a default strategy. Turns out, I was wrong. We learn resilience much quicker than I expected. It soon became clear that five failure–resilience strategy–reflection journal entries (i.e., repeat this practice five times) were enough to provide a tipping point to propel women to lean into resilience instead of being consumed with failure. When asked about the most important take-away from my workshops, many women cite these resilience strategies.

PRESS PAUSE AND CHANGE THE TAPE

First, at the risk of dating myself, let's make sure we all understand what I mean by a tape. Remember when we used to play music on eight-track tapes? And then cassette tapes? The beauty of music tapes was that you could get to the end of the song, press rewind, and play it again. And again. And as my parents can testify, again.

Thoughts work the same way. In addition to the self-defeating thoughts that spring up when we make a mistake, we also have other negative tapes running around in our heads. These tapes work like cassette tapes or VHS recordings that play repeatedly, sometimes with little provocation and always without our consent. Sometimes it's just a dreary Monday morning and the end of the semester is nowhere in sight. I am tired, discouraged, and lack my usual motivation and deter-mination. In my head I hear "You cannot do this. You'll never make it. Go ahead and quit." And if I don't press pause, and change that negative thought tape quickly, I will quit.

In my case, one of the tapes that keeps playing when I make a mistake or fail is, "Jane, you are stupid, fat, and ugly and you will never amount to much." Not exactly words of inspiration, much less forgiveness or resilience. In my work with coaching women to build resilience, women have shared soul crushing tapes that play in their head whenever they fail. One tape came from a Black woman who was told she needed to be three times better than anyone else because she was Black, and she was female. Three times better than anyone else? I've felt crushed under the lie that, as a woman, I needed to be twice as good as the men around me. How could any human manage to be three times better???

Another tape came from a successful lawyer who shared with me that, whenever she failed, she was reminded, via the tape that played in her head, that she'd be so much prettier if she lost weight. What?!? She was beautiful as she was. Why would any woman think she needed to lose weight to be pretty and, consequently, successful??? And what does physical appearance have to do with legal skills???? And yet, as women, we live under the burden of these lies daily.

Even microaggressions can become tapes that stay stuck in our heads. A former woman athlete recalled how a man on her team insisted it was "easy for women to become Division I student-athletes," totally undermining all the work, time, energy, and pain she endured to earn that D-1 scholarship and a starting berth on her team. And the fact that she could recall this barb at a moment's notice, long after she was finished competing, tells me this demeaning tape had played in her head repeatedly.

These negative and dysfunctional thoughts are especially detrimental because they work like tapes in our heads. Repeating negative thoughts that instinctively pop up when you fail is not good—in fact, it makes the issue worse because now you're stuck in a rut of thinking, and you are reinforcing and memorizing beliefs that make you feel less than or unworthy. Think about how you memorized your mom's phone number when you were in kindergarten. You kept repeating it to yourself over and over again until you would never forget it. The same thing happens with the negative thoughts we keep telling ourselves. We need to change the tape from one of negativity and despair to encouragement and support.

The tape that plays in my head is that I am "stupid, fat, and ugly," and implies that "I will never amount to much." Without intentional thinking, that tape played in my head for years every time I fell short of my expectations for myself. I have to admit, the tape is still there, and in my experience, try as I might, the tape does not get erased. However, I have learned to recognize when it starts to play—like recognizing the first bars of a popular song—and crowd it out with positive thoughts. But that takes practice. Lots of practice. And I admit I have to practice drowning out negative tapes daily. And neuroscience tells us our brain naturally hangs on to negativity while positivity slides off unless we make a concerted effort to savor it. But here's the good news. It's not easy, and it's not fun. But if I can do it, you can do it. Here's how.

There are four steps to start changing the tape.

1. After you've identified the negative tape running wild in your head after a mistake or failure, ask yourself who put those tapes in your head? Hint: it wasn't you. It may have been so long ago, and you've played the tapes to yourself so frequently, you have forgotten, or never considered who put that tape in your head the first time. It could have been a parent, a coach, a boss, a sibling, a teammate, a teacher, or a bully; the important thing is identifying where the tape originated.

2. The purpose in identifying the tape's origin is not to seek revenge, or even to practice forgiveness. Both are challenging. Be gentle with yourself and give grace to the other person. No judgment. When in doubt, I like to think the best of people. My guess is that the individual who kept calling me lazy as a youngster was trying to motivate me—no matter how convoluted that sounds. I don't think motivation works that way—at least not for me—but I will give this individual the benefit of the doubt and assume their misguided soul-crushing tape was intended to be helpful rather than hurtful. And right now, I'm working on me, not them, so keep your focus.

3. After identifying the individual, ask yourself if this person currently has influence over you today. Hint: the bully in first grade is long gone and has moved on (likely to bully other people), but the destructive tape remains in your head. Does this person really have power and influence over your life at this point? They likely did in the past, but my guess is while that power has diminished, the negative tapes they instilled are still playing.

4. A funny example is from my second-grade teacher. That's right, second grade which was a long, long time ago. My second-grade teacher

said I had terrible penmanship. (Seriously?!? Who gives a rip about penmanship—not writing, penmansh p. Ugh.) My penmanship was so bad, I was selected to choose the classmate with the best penmanship. The teacher's rationale, which she explained to the class, was that my penmanship—shouldn't we at least call it pen-personship???—was so bad, I was not in the consideration set. So I got to pick the winner. As you might guess, as I progressed through school, my penmanship never really improved, but it didn't matter (take that, second grade teacher who will remain anonymous to spare her embarrassment even though I rememb er her name) because papers were required to be typed. Keep in mind, this was before Word had been invented. I carried the ugly penmanship defeating thought throughout my college career until a favorite English professor, who also had terrible writing, proclaimed that bad handwriting is a sign of intelligence and gave the undecipherable handwriting of medical doctors as an example. Hooray. I was finally free of this burden. Every time self-incriminating and defeating thoughts about my messy handwriting started to creep in, I rem nded myself—and others if they asked—that bad handwriting is a sign of intelligence. And yes, as my students can attest, my handwriting hasn't improved with age. And it's OK. My second-grade teacher no longer has influence over my life, or my thoughts about my worthiness.

Once you've identified who put this tape in your head, ask yourself "Is it true?" or "Is it helpful?" Is it motivating you or dispiriting you so you want to quit? Does it build you up or tear you down? Energize you or defeat you? You get the idea.

Reflect—Does this person really have power and influence over your life at this point? They likely did in the past, but my guess is while that power has diminished, the negative tapes they instilled are still playing.

In my case, I have a PhD—I must not be stupid. However, to give you an example of how insidious and prevalent this tape was in my head, I was halfway through my PhD program (i.e., honor student in college, MBA, admission to law school and success in graduate school) before I realized the individual who claimed to be responsible for my academic success because I was stupid, was no longer around. In fact, this individual had been out of my academic life well before high school and had no claim on my academic achievement. It was a major breakthrough to realize I might actually be smart enough to finish a PhD program. And I did. As for fat—my physician tells me my weight range is healthy and I don't make a living as a model so I'm good looking enough. Take that. Be kind to yourself. As an alternative to is it true, ask yourself is this tape helpful?

But the acid test is one of parenting and friendship depending upon your life stage. Ask yourself, would you say these mean things to your best friend or to your children? When I asked myself this question, I was mortified. I would never say these things to my daughters; it would devastate them. So then, I had to ask, why do I say it to myself? Here is the acid test when evaluating tapes. If you wouldn't say it to your best friend or child, you have no business saying it to yourself. Game over.

Reflect—Would you ever say the negative thoughts you tell yourself, to your best friend or child?

CHANGE THE TAPE

It is important to note that in my experience, it is next to impossible to erase the tape. I wish I could. I can't even stop the tape. But I have learned to drown it out with positive thoughts. The negative tapes are still there—they always will be—but now I know when they start to play, I don't have to listen to them anymore. I can drown them out.

The other thing I've noticed is that the tape is more likely to play when I am tired or hungry—in other words, my resources are low. When not fulfilling my basic needs—food and sleep—I don't have the energy to stop the tape or drown it out. But through experience and practice, I am now able to recognize my physical limitations and be aware that the tape is likely to play because I'm lacking the necessary energy to stomp it down.

Since it is next to impossible to erase the tape or stop it from playing, the best method I've found for dealing with these self-defeating thoughts is to crowd them out with thoughts that are helpful. It is as if someone is singing an annoying song that you can't stand, and they won't stop. So, you sing louder and block out their song. In a sense, you crowd out the negative by overshadowing it with something else.

CROWDING OUT THE TAPE

Practice—Practice using positive quotations, images, songs, mantras, smells, etc. to crowd out negative thoughts. How did that work? What are your favorite "go to" strategies to squash those negative thoughts when they start to bubble up?

What are the things you say to yourself when you are at your best? Or what are the things your best friend says to you to build you up? Think of these things. Here are a couple of examples other women and I use to replace negative thoughts with empowering ones.

* Empowering songs—One of my favorites is "I'm an overcomer." I have no idea who sings it or the rest of the lyrics but singing "I'm an overcomer" silences demeaning thoughts.

* Smells—Our olfactory sense (smell) is one of the oldest reflexes embedded in our minds. Even if we can't identify the smell, we associate it with memories—both good and bad. Some people find the smell of pine trees to be reassuring (holiday memories?). Others like to remember the smell of chocolate chip cookies baking (fond

memories of home?). When one of my daughters was away at college, she would head to the department store fragrance counter to smell my perfume and bring back good memories (I hope!) of Mom and home.

* Given my love for written language, I have various mantras or inspirational sayings that I use regularly. When I'm discouraged and the negative tape starts to play, I remind myself that "You can be pitiful or you can be powerful, but you can't be both. Which do you choose?" When phrased that way, even someone like me who loves to throw a good pity party for herself, chooses power. "I choose power." And I get back to work.

* Another one of my favorite mantras is "I am confident and determined. I am not fearful nor discouraged, for the Lord my God is with me wherever I go." (based on Joshua 1:9). Take that! I cannot count the times I have repeated all of these mantras to myself to overshadow negative thoughts.

Changing the tape—or practicing replacing negative, self-defeating thoughts with positive thoughts, is one of the hardest things I've done. I have to practice it every day. Because I've been practicing for years, and I mean more than twenty years . . . , I've gotten better at shutting down the negative thoughts. But they still come up and I still have to take active steps to intentionally overshadow them. So don't get discouraged if you can't get the tape changed right away. Keep practicing. Be intentional about what you choose to think and the thoughts you allow in your mind. You may not be able to control what other people think about you, but you CAN control what you think about you. Keep it positive.

To help me intentionally turn my attention away from negative thoughts and instead, focus on thoughts that build me up, I collect inspirational sayings and hang them where you can see them. How hard is it to change the tape? Hard. I write my mantras on index cards that I have all over my house—taped to my bathroom mirror, in my car, on my computer, in my purse, my backpack, etc. etc. etc. Make index cards of the inspirations that keep your thinking on track and post them everywhere.

Because this strategy has helped me so much and because so many people are discouraged and hurting, I like to actively share positive inspirations with others who need encouragement. We are not the only people who get discouraged. Think about the inspirations that help you make it through tough times and share them with someone else. Who else needs to be inspired? I love sending fr ends who are going through a rough time a notecard containing an incex card and an inspirational saying on it. I've had students return to my office upon graduation and show me the torn, dilapidated index card with the positive affirmation I gave them. It works. And this activity bears double consequences; by making someone else feel better, you feel better too.

On a more general level, I like to spread inspiration throughout my environment—where I work, teach, volunteer and at home. Each Women in Sales class starts with an "inspiration of day." Students bring in inspirations and share them with the class. We post them on the wall (large Post-It notes) so students can see them throughout the class period. Similarly, at the dog shelter, it can get very discouraging to see precious pups neglected, abused, and abandoned. To keep ourselves as enthusiastic as the forgiving dogs we help, volunteers hang positive Post-It notes like "You are making a difference" throughout the kennels to drown out discouragement. Being intentional about what you think and attend to has big payoffs.

FAILURE IS AN EVENT, NOT A PERSON

RESILIENCE STRATEGIES—REFRAMING PAST REGRETS

One of my personal favorite resilience strategies to use for small failures or mistakes is to remind myself that "failure is an event, not a person." We've already established that we tend to beat ourselves up when we fail. In many cases, we take it a step further and spiral the failure down to an endless abyss—kind of like Dante's *Inferno*—where not only do we beat ourselves up, we see our mishap as an end to civilization as we know it. I have watched young women in my office spiral down from a less than perfect performance review, to imagining themselves getting fired, never being employed again, and living homeless on the streets. A bit dramatic? Yes. Have I done it? Yes. And I've watched other women do it too. This strategy helps you reframe and see the failure as the event that it is, instead of a measure of your self-worth. The failure is one event; it does not make you, the person, a failure.

Instead of acknowledging that the failure was only a misstep in a long, life journey, what happens all too frequently is that we let the failure loom large and spiral out of control. My knee-jerk reaction is that I'm a failure. No good. Done for. Game over. Note the emphasis is on me—as if this one mistake reflects a gaping character flaw. It's not my behavior that I'm questioning. I'm doubting that I'm good enough. My first thought is "I'm a failure." And the subsequent thoughts spiral downward after that.

We need to rethink the "I am a failure." Instead of allowing the mistake to imply a character flaw (I'm a failure), reframe the failure as an event. Upon reflection, I fear I said something stupid in a meeting. Note the role that fear plays here. In reality, do I know for sure, that other faculty in the meeting thought I made a stupid comment? No. Yet, upon reflection, I assume and fear, (probably irrationally), that everyone thought my comment was stupid and I am stupid and I start beating myself up. Will I ever learn to keep my mouth shut? The answer is probably no and I'm glad. We need to keep speaking up. But I digress. Darn. It's OK to swear and/or be disappointed. But remind yourself, I am still smart, I am still kind, I am still compassionate, and I am a good leader. I made a comment that maybe I shouldn't have said. Now move on.

I would use a similar approach to disciplining my young daughters—and to be clear, I'm talking about my good days when I had my act together. Trust me, there were many not-so-good days as a mother when I disciplined out of frustration, impatience, or lack of energy. We're not going there today. But when my patience and self-control were intact and my daughters misbehaved, my loving (and best) response was "I love you very much, but your behavior is unacceptable." I made a clear separation from themselves and their behavior. They were still good people. Always have been, always will be. But their behavior was unacceptable. I'm hoping you had similar discipline as well.

The hardest thing about coaching resilience is practicing what I teach. One of my favorite sayings is, "We teach best what we most need to learn," (Richard Bach) and resilience is no exception. While directing a center for professional selling, I was tasked with producing a city-wide event bringing together regional sales leaders. Keep in mind, like many women in the process of building their careers, in addition to directing the sales center, I was also coaching our sales team, teaching a full load of classes, and playing mom to three teenage daughters. I hyperventilate just thinking about how overwhelmed I felt at that time of my life. In my haste to get the invitations and publicity out to our constituents, I rapidly glanced at the proofs, and sent them out for distribution. All was well and I had moved onto the next task when I received a phone call from the keynote speaker. Turns out the daughter of a leader in our field happened to also live in Cincinnati (what are the chances) and saw the advance publicity touting, among others, her father whose name I had misspelled. The keynote was upset—what does this misspelling say about the quality of the event—and I was mortified when the error was pointed out to me. I know how to spell this name; I was rushed and I made a mistake. I truly thought my career had ended. When I went running to my supervisor expecting to be fired, she calmly reiterated that I made a mistake and that we can reprint and retract with the correct spelling. In fact, her concern was that this was yet another indicator I was too busy (note to self—re-read section on busyness) and that everyone makes mistakes. Error was corrected; problem solved. But I could not let myself off the hook so easily. I continued to mentally berate myself for making a stupid spelling error and imagined that no one would ever want me in a leadership position again. Then I remembered what I tell other women in my position—failure is an event, not a person. I started reminding myself that I am smart, I am hard-working, I am a good leader and I made a spelling mistake. Failure is an event, not a person.

I find "Failure is an event, not a person" convenient to use for small failures, setbacks or mistakes. The fact that I have memorized it gives you an indication of how frequently I use it.

Practice—Next time you fail, or make a mistake, remind yourself that failure is not a measure of your self-worth. In addition to reframing the failure as an event, highlight the attributes that make you special.

This truly is one of my favorite go-to resilience strategies. When my children were little and I was in a good place—i.e., calm, focused, patient, rested, and not hungry—which didn't happen as often as I wished it had—and one of my daughters misbehaved, I'd separate their behavior from their identity and worthiness. My reprimand, which I sure I read somewhere in some child psychology book delivered in a soft, calm voice (I'm in my good place-remember?) would remind them how much I loved them but their behavior was inappropriate, unacceptable, unsuitable, or fill-in-the-blank. This approach to discipline seemed to work and it made me feel better about chastising them. "I love you very much. But it's your behavior that is unacceptable," sounds so much kinder than the usual "What the heck were you thinking?" Etc. etc. that I slipped into when my children misbehaved and I was not in a good place. And in case you're worried, they all turned out fine.

Another fun story about this strategy was shared by a former Women in Sales student. While she was an award-winning, straight-A honor student, her younger brother was not. And as the family sat around the dinner table one night with her younger brother beating himself up for an evidently stupid mistake (I have no idea what he did—but whatever it was, he knew he made a mistake and was beating himself up for it), my student said, "Listen You made a mistake. But failure is an event, not a person. You are still a kind, caring, compassion-ate human being and you will make a positive contribution to society. Now move forward." And he did. He made it to college and took Women in Sales.

REFRAME: SEE FAILURE AS COURAGE

As previously mentioned, we all have our favorite, go to resilience strategy and, I must confess, this one is a favorite of mine. The idea behind
this strategy is to see failure as courage. Even though the outcome may
have not been what you wanted, the fact that you tried is worth cele-
brating. Pat yourself on the back for having the courage to take a risk
and try something new.

This strategy is based on the work of one of my favorite authors and
leadership guru, Brené Brown. She frequently quotes Teddy Roosevelt
who knew a thing or two about loss and resilience. Teddy Roosevelt's
wife and mother both died in the same house on the same day. Can
you imagine? He went from the first floor of his home, watched his
wife die after giving birth to their daughter, Alice Roosevelt Longworth,
and then went up to the third floor of his home to be with his mother
while she died. I honestly can't fathom the depth of pain he must have
felt. He then went out West for a couple of years to heal his soul. He
set a timer on his pity party—two years—and the rest is history. (For
a more detailed description of the deaths and the impact they had on
Roosevelt's life, read *The Bully Pulpit* by Doris Kearns Goodwin). When
Teddy Roosevelt talks about loss, pain, and failure, I take him at his word.
So does Brené Brown who frequently cites the words below. As Teddy
Roosevelt writes:

*"It's not the critic who counts; not the man who points
out how the strong man stumbles or where the doer of
deeds could have done them better. The credit belongs
to the man who is actually in the arena, whose face
is marred by dust and sweat and blood, who strives
valiantly; who errs, who comes short again and again,
because there is not effort without error . . . and who at
the worst, if he fails, at least fails while daring greatly. . . ."*

I don't know about you, but that quotation gives me goosebumps. Of
course, I'd like to change all the references about men daring greatly to
gender neutral nouns but, given the period in which it was written, I'll

give Teddy a pass on that one. This quotation should inspire everyone to get out there and fail. The crime is not in the failing, it's in the not trying.

This quotation explains why I have a lot of respect for people who run for political office. Setting political opinions aside, it takes great courage to run for public office. I'm a chicken and so embarrassed about the possibility of losing, that I've not applied for awards, fellowships, and jobs because I was afraid of what people would think of me if I failed to achieve my aspirations. When someone enters a political race, unless they are running unopposed, someone is going to lose. And in politics, losing is a front-page newspaper story. Not only must politicians contend with the disappointment and expense of losing a political contest, they also have their failure broadcast on national TV. I'd rather die.

Teddy Roosevelt and his fan, Brené Brown, helped change the way I looked at failure. Instead of being ashamed of failing, which was all I knew, the Roosevelt quotation turns that upside down. Teddy Roosevelt and Brené Brown tell us to be proud of our failure, because, even though it didn't go as we expected, we had the courage to try. And I couldn't agree more.

I used this strategy a couple of years ago when I applied for an associate dean's position at my school. In hindsight, thank goodness I did not get the job. It would have been terrible for me (my heart is in teaching, not administrating) and it would not have been good for the college. But at the time, I thought I wanted to be an associate dean and I dutifully sent in my application. To my embarrassment, I didn't even get a first-round interview.

Let me clarify that for you. In the search committees I've been on, we always grant inside candidates a courtesy interview. Within the committee we may have no intention of seriously considering an insider's application, but if it comes from an inside candidate, we give a first-round courtesy interview. I didn't even get that! How embarrassing. I was rejected right off the bat. Maybe the committee reached the same conclusion I eventually reached—I would not have made a good associate dean. But the least they could have done was give me a first-round courtesy interview.

I was crushed and embarrassed. Keep in mind, only the search committee, my family (who also thought applying for the job was a terrible idea), and a few very close friends knew I applied. It wasn't like the world knew I failed to get an interview, much less a job. And yet, I thought everyone on campus was mocking my failure. The truth is, no one knew and no one cared. My interpretation of the rejection was that my colleagues were so unimpressed with my credentials and experience that they didn't even consider me a worthy candidate.

My thoughts started spiraling downward. "They must think I'm an idiot." "What a joke—they didn't even want to take the time to talk to me." "They are probably laughing at me now." And the thoughts go down from there. Once again, who knows what the committee was thinking. For all I know, my application got lost in technology. I don't know. But instead of admitting I can't read minds or overhear confidential committee meetings, I assumed I had failed: miserably and publicly.

Then I remembered the "see failure as courage" strategy and started to reframe the experience from one of embarrassing failure to one of pride. That's right. I reevaluated the process and decided to be proud that I had the courage to apply for the position. I had never applied for an administrative position in academia before. Good for me for trying something new. While other faculty members were standing around the copy machine, complaining, I had the courage to apply for the position. Instead of sitting around moaning about the problem, I wrote my job letter outlining where the college was falling short and what steps I would take to change it. Instead of complaining in the hallway, I had the courage to step up and say what I would do to change. Instead of being ashamed, I became proud that I took a risk. Maybe I failed, but at least I tried. I think Teddy R. would have been proud of me too.

I love it when women use this strategy because it really reinforces the power of taking a risk and trying something new. Working closely with young women, it is impossible to not notice the impact that relationships—often with the other gender—have on their well-being and mental health. Many a conversation has been had about a failed relationship—usually with a boyfriend, but sometimes with a roommate or a sorority sister. And while I don't begin to understand the mating rituals of this younger generation, I do remember the pain of waiting to be chosen—for a prom date, a night out, or an intramural basketball team.

Consequently, I was curious and proud when a woman told me about her experience asking a guy out. She had been eyeing him and had worked with him on a couple of projects. She threw caution to the wind and drummed up the courage to ask him out instead of waiting for him to ask her. What a nice option. And I bet there are shy, introverted men out there who would love it if a woman asked them out, so they didn't have to. But in this case, his answer was no. She was rejected and failed in her request. But instead of being down and out, and feeling like a failure, she decided to see failure as courage. Even though she was hesitant to ask a boy out, she did it anyway and was proud of herself for asking. I couldn't agree more. She did it. And even though this one didn't have the ending she hoped for, she also didn't spend hours waiting for the phone to ring and hoping it was him. She asked, she got her answer, and she moved on. Good for her. And FYI–she is now in law school.

In addition to the previous example, women I mentor tend to use this strategy when applying for stretch jobs. They may not get the job, but every time they are proud of themselves for applying. And the good news is I have no idea when they finally succeed. The power comes from getting over the failure. If you can do that, the success will come.

When you put yourself out there and become vulnerable, public "failure" is embarrassing. Campaigning for a government office and not winning the election is humiliating. Applying for a stretch job is scary but, if you don't apply, the answer is always no. Reframe "failure" as courage. It's easy to stay on the sidelines and criticize others, like the Monday morning armchair quarterback. But you had the courage to actually be in the ring. Be proud of yourself and pat yourself on the back. You go, girl!

STAY POSITIVE IN THE PROCESS

Full disclosure. I struggle with this strategy. I am not a naturally optimistic person. Probably one of the reasons I work with salespeople is because I love their optimism. Have you ever met a depressed salesperson? Probably not. Because if you are a Debby Downer, you will never make it in the world of sales. No customer wants to be around a depressed salesperson—they want to be with salespeople who are positive, likable, and fun to be around.

Unfortunately, I tend to be pessimistic by nature. Only through practice and desperation have I learned to be more optimistic than is natural to me. Turns out, nobody likes to be around pessimistic people either and part of attracting clients is endless optimism. If left to my own thoughts, I can imagine everything that can go wrong and fully expect it to do so. It is a challenge for me to stay positive. And staying positive while things are not going well is an even bigger struggle. But this strategy has proven to be effective in teaching me, and other women, to be resilient and confident in the moment instead of feeling defeated.

The strategy of "staying positive in the process" requires you to stop those negative, self-defeating thoughts while you're in the moment and instead, be optimistic that you can do this. For example, take me and technology. Face it—given my age and aptitude, technology and I do not get along. The IT department at my office sees me as job security—as long as I'm around, they will have jobs because I am so inept at technology. So, you can imagine what happened when the powers-that-be decided to switch our main platform from a program I had finally learned to a new "upgraded" platform. I was just finally getting comfortable—and competent—using the old one and we switched to a new one. Are you kidding me?!? My first encounters with the new system were less than successful and, truth be told, much of that was my fault. Instead of being creative and looking at the platform as a different learning tool, I chose to grumble and complain that it was too hard to learn. Once I reframed the challenge from "I will never be able to learn this" perspective, to "it's good for me to learn new things," adapting to the new version became easier. Staying positive in the process with an I-can-do-this mentality made the learning process easier. Staying stuck in the this-is-impossible mindset made the learning painstakingly frustrating.

The key to using this strategy is having the wherewithal to execute it while you're in the process of failing. Instead of giving into the I'm-never-going-to-make-it or I-can't-do-this mindset, you instead give yourself a little internal pep talk and remind yourself that you can do this. Make no mistake, it takes self-control to stay positive in the process because it's so much easier to just give up. But with practice, you will learn to stay positive.

One example when a businesswoman used this strategy effectively, a seemingly minor incident, resonated with me. The woman and her friends were meeting for dinner, and she had the perfect (there's that word again!) place in mind. Unfortunately for her, her friends wanted a different restaurant, and she was unable to persuade them to change their vote. So, she failed to get the restaurant of her choice and instead found herself stuck eating at a different place.

I've been there and it's not pretty. Instead of being grateful that I am eating out with my friends, I usually brood the entire evening about not getting my choice and, if possible, try to make others as miserable as possible as punishment for not choosing my restaurant. Clearly, I'm not my best self in this moment. Instead of behaving like me and insisting on having a miserable time, this woman chose to stay positive in the process. She writes about how she focused on her gratitude toward her friends, the warm conversation, and the time they were able to spend together. By staying positive throughout the evening, she reports that she enjoyed herself. The restaurant choice was irrelevant. And yes, she had a good time.

Reflect—*Can you think of a time when you were not positive in the moment and, in fact, succumbed to negative, self-defeating thoughts while you were engaged in the activity? How did it go?*

While that is a seemingly minor incident with minimal consequences, other women and I have employed this strategy during events
with more significant consequences. A former president of a premier
business group for women in our organization and I made a proposal
to our bosses' boss. We were proposing the creation a space in the
business building dedicated to women. When it was time to meet with
the big boss, a man of course, we were ready. My colleague had created
a breathtakingly beautiful Prezi slide deck and I had the script, so we
started our presentation. As the presentation progressed, I kept watching the big boss for his reaction. Nothing. He wasn't smiling, he wasn't
nodding his head or asking questions. With my typical pessimistic perspective, I quickly assumed that he hated us, he hated our idea, and he
wanted us out of his office. That negative, self-defeating (note that the
man had not yet said a word) mindset was ready to spell defeat even if
it wasn't correct.

To his credit, and I will always be grateful to him for this moment,
he stopped the presentation, and told us about his processing style.
He is a thinker—no surprise given his responsibilities and academic
background—who processes information slowly and intentionally. He
warned us to not interpret his lack of questions as a negative assessment; he was processing the information. His interruption allowed
me to refocus and stay positive in the process. We still had a chance
of getting his approval and my negative, self-defeating thoughts were
inappropriate. We finished our proposal with questions and accolades
from not only him, but from others in the room as well. In the end, we
didn't get the space we wanted. But everyone was impressed with our
proposal and gave it serious consideration. I'm glad I stayed positive and
didn't give into defeat.

I have found young women use this strategy successfully in
group job interviews and at career fairs for entry level positions. One
woman wrote about being in a job interview with a prestigious Fortune 500 company. The interview began with everyone going around
the circle and introducing themselves and their graduate degree. She
found herself surrounded by Ivy League students, and students from
reputable Big Ten business schools. While I like to think of the university she attended as the Harvard of the Midwest, most people would
disagree, and this woman could feel her confidence shrinking with
each introduction from others vying for the job. And this was just the

beginning of the interview. Instead of giving into the self-defeating negative thoughts, she decided to stay positive in the process. She reminded herself that she had earned the right to be at the interview. If this company hadn't wanted her, or didn't think she was capable, they wouldn't have invited her. She decided she was as good as anyone else and stayed positive. This story does have a happy ending. There were 12 job candidates and two job offers: one of which went to this woman. Cha-ching. Way to go.

Young women I mentor find this strategy helpful at networking events. I admit, as a card-carrying introvert, networking events are not my favorite activity. Truth be told, I avoid them like the plague. And yet, I know they are important and essential in today's world. As much as I don't like it, I go. I have to admit I usually have a good time and meet interesting people I normally wouldn't come in contact with. But to young women—who have been admonished since kindergarten to not talk to strangers and who are adept at texting but avoid in-person and phone conversations—a networking event is as scary as it gets.

To help women beginning their careers to get over their fear of networking, we practice introductions, and develop questions to ask others at the event. I've even gone so far as to stage a mock networking event—using my husband as a stranger—to help women become comfortable meeting new people. In spite of all that, the women I coach are nervous about attending and would pass if I gave them a way out. Not.

One woman recounted that she bravely approached someone at a networking event and was basically ignored. She was nervous and didn't want to go in the first place, and the first person she talked to basically brushed her aside to speak with someone else. Talk about feeling like a failure. In her words, she was ready to quit and go home, resigned that she was a failure at networking.

But then she remembered this resilience strategy—stay positive in the process. She reminded herself that only one person didn't want to talk with her and that there were thirty-five other people at the event who did. She put a smile on her face and, instead of walking out the door, she went up to the next person and introduced herself. This story ends on a happy note. She connected with an individual who become instrumental in her career. Without the resilience she needed to bounce back after the first failure, she never would have had the confidence and courage to try again. And it worked.

In a group meeting where everyone is presenting ideas, it can be natural to generate unfavorable comparisons and feel inadequate. It may be OK to have those thoughts after the meeting, but during the meeting it is essential to stay positive and remind yourself that you have earned your right to be there, and you have a right to be heard. If trying a new task (technology) the process goes smoother if you focus on the benefits of learning a new tool instead of complaining about how much you hate technology. Stay positive in the process.

Practice—Practice small. Next time you don't get your way— whether that be your choice of restaurant, movie, or game—decide that you are going to stay positive in the process and enjoy the event. How did you feel? What happened?

SET A TIMER ON THE PITY PARTY

In addition to my role as Queen of Failure, I also consider myself the Princess of Pity Parties. I love a good pity party and am an expert at hosting. Throughout my many pity parties, for myself of course, I have lamented that no one works harder than I do, no one appreciates what I do, no one has sacrificed more than I have, and the list goes on and on. If this were interactive, right about now I'd cue the violins to start playing a funeral dirge. And yes please, I'd like some cheese to go with my whine. Thank you very much. You get the idea. And judging from the number of women who report using this resilience strategy, I am not the only one who loves a good pity party.

There is nothing inherently wrong with occasionally feeling sorry for yourself. I get it. Sometimes a good cry and a pint of Graeter's ice cream just helps. What I'm talking about is wallowing in the self–pity. Like hogs wallowing in mud, the problem with wallowing is that you get stuck. And when you're stuck, you're ruminating, you're beating yourself up, and you're not moving forward to take advantage of opportunities that come your way.

Let me share an extreme example of an excessive pity party that droned on for way too long. At one point in my career, I was turned down for a promotion. (Friendly reminder, I tend to be an overachieving perfectionist so this failure hit especially hard.) There are a lot of ugly backstories, but that's not what I want to focus on. My focus here is how I reacted to that failure. The cause of the failure was a result of several things I could not control. But the one thing I could control was my reaction to the failure, and eventually I did, but it was way too long in coming and not one of my best moments.

Keep in mind, this took place long before I knew anything about resilience. No one had ever talked to me about resilience and I'm not even sure I knew the word. The concept of getting over failure was foreign to me; I thought failure signaled the end. After getting turned down I floundered for a year-and-a-half feeling sorry for myself—poor me, it's so unfair (and yes it was—but that's not the issue), how could they do this after all I've done for them, etc. etc. etc. You get the drift. I continued to stay stuck, seething about the decision, until a kind soul—interestingly enough, a man—pulled me aside. He said, "Jane, read the letter. They're not asking for much. Do what they are asking and apply again."

Holy cow! The lightbulb went on. I was spending all my cognitive and emotional energy debating whether I should appeal the decision, file a lawsuit, leave for another school, or hire an arsonist. (Note: I wasn't really serious about the arsonist but on especially angry days, the thought of causing damage did creep in and, fortunately, out of my mind.) The thought of reapplying for a promotion never occurred to me. Seriously. Doing what the committee asked (which was easy) and applying again, never crossed my mind.

Once rejected, I jumped to the conclusion, meant always rejected. Talk about a lack of resilience. Crown me the poster child. I think about this example and wonder how many other women have taken a "no" to mean "never," when it really meant "not yet." And to be clear, it's not fair when we have to reapply while mediocre men sail through. But only when we reapply, and get the promotion or appointment, will we accumulate the power needed to change the system. We need to keep reapplying so our daughters and granddaughters won't have to.

Turns out I'm not alone in my reticence to reapply after rejection. Recent research found that women are 40% less likely than men to reapply for a leadership position once they have been turned down. Ouch. Clearly, I am not alone. And, as was true in my case, there are other external factors that are likely neither fair nor just which come into play in the initial rejection. I get that. There are a lot of people who don't want women in leadership positions and set double standards, explicitly or implicitly, when evaluating women for promotion. True. And that needs to change. But cultural and social change is a long time coming. Meanwhile, we need to work on what we can control—how we react to failure. If we lack resilience and quit after one rejection, they've won and we're done.

I still believe in the benefit of taking time to mourn your losses. Failure is a loss. While waiting to hear if you got the job, you imagine the apartment, the city, and lifestyle that awaits you with this new job. A job rejection, or failure to get the offer, is the loss of that dream. While waiting to hear if your manuscript is accepted, you fantasize about telling all your friends and family about your publication. A rejection means that dream is over. And the loss of a dream deserves to be mourned. The key is to not get stuck—for days, or for weeks, or for months—in mourning.

To allow yourself time to grieve the loss, but not get stuck in a pity party, use a timer to set a specific amount of time that you allow yourself to grieve. How much time? My recommendation is to make the amount of time commiserate with the level of loss or failure. For small losses—an internship rejection, a negative interaction with a customer, or a less-than-perfect grade—I tend to keep the pity party small and set the timer for anywhere from five minutes to two hours. For more severe losses, I may allow myself a day to mourn. But no more than a day. Experiment and choose the time that works for you.

For example, one morning I received a tearful email from a woman I had been mentoring. She explained that her boyfriend (re: the man of her dreams) had broken up with her the night before and she was too distraught to attend a meeting that afternoon. I understood. Her relationship with her boyfriend had failed and, along with it, her dreams for the future that she had envisioned with him. Imagine my pleasant surprise when she showed up for the meeting, albeit red eyes instead of her usual sparkly self, but sitting in her seat and participating as always. When I expressed curiosity that she attended given the earlier email, she told me that she put a timer on the pity party. She set a timer for three hours—most of the morning—and cried her eyes out. When the timer went off, she was done crying. She blew her nose, wiped her eyes and declared it time to move on with her life. She was proud of herself for not wallowing in her pain and for showing up for herself. And I was proud of her too.

I saw a variation of this strategy while leading a corporate workshop on resilience. One of the women executives in the group noted that, when she calls her mom to complain about the frustration of working in a predominately male organization (need I say more?), her mom gives her five minutes to vent. That's it. The executive gets five minutes to whine to her mom and feel sorry for herself. After five minutes, her mom stops the conversation and redirects to something positive. I have a sneaky suspicion that this mother was intentionally or unintentionally instrumental in helping her daughter build the resilience responsible for her success in the corporate ranks. Would that we could all be fortunate enough to have wise mothers.

I have also used this strategy when helping women navigate their careers. An acquaintance called me one day asking for career advice. She spent the first twenty minutes of our conversation talking about her current job and the toxic environment she dealt with. I did not disagree and, in fact, concurred with her that it was time for her to move on from her current position. We talked about her resume and then she started rehashing the same destructive incidents that she's already stated and I'd already heard. I said, enough! And reminded her about putting a timer on the pity party. I gently chided her—you can spend 15 minutes droning on about the soul-sucking negative place you work, or you could be writing a job letter. Which will serve you better? As we ended our conversation, she promised to restrict the pity party to five minutes a day and devote the rest of her time job hunting. And, last I heard, she landed a great sales job with a company that appreciates her. A good win.

Throughout this guidebook, I encourage you to practice failing with small stuff so you're prepared when larger losses occur. While, thank goodness, I don't have to use these resilience strategies often for major failures, I do need to employ them occasionally, and this is one I use for failure and loss. There was a time when my husband needed to step away from his position and it hurt the whole family. While we were grieving the loss of life as we knew it, there were days when I could barely get out of bed, much less try to accomplish something meaningful at work. Fortunately, I had a flexible schedule and was able to take a grieving day. Keep in mind it was a grieving day—not a week, not a month, not even two days. More than one day and we're talking about depression. But I would take one day, sit on my back deck, stare into space because I couldn't move, and then go to bed. The funny thing, that I cannot explain other than the grace of God, is that somehow allowing myself one day to grieve made it possible for me to bounce back the following day. I was always afraid that allowing an entire day of grief would evolve into weeks of self-pity. It never happened. By giving myself a day, I got back to business the next day.

Another similar strategy that is closely related to this one is to postpone the pity party. When something bad happens and you want to burst into tears, instead, promise yourself that you can cry in the shower later, but you need to hold it together now. I've used this one multiple times. At one job, an efficient but socially awkward manager interrupted me as I was about to walk into a meeting I had to lead. He informed me that my position had been eliminated and I needed to start looking for another position. As much as I wanted to burst into tears, I had a meeting to lead and people who depended on me. So, I promised myself I could cry in the car on my way home from work. But right now, I had a job to do and I needed to get in there and do it. The funny thing about postponing the pity party, is that by the time I got around to feeling sorry for myself, I didn't feel like crying anymore. I didn't need the pity party. And BTW, I kept my job.

Please note that this strategy—like all of the strategies—doesn't always work for everyone. Setting a timer on the pity party is a favorite among women I coach. But it is also one that doesn't always work for everyone in every instance. In some cases, you may set a timer on the pity party, but when the timer goes off, you're still thinking and ruminating about the failure. If this is the case, try a different resilience strategy; putting on a timer on the pity party is not working for you in this case. In instances like this, I suggest trying the "Press pause and change the tape" strategy. It's clear your mind is stuck focusing on the failure so you need to press pause and change the tape to something positive.

It's OK to feel bad when you fail but put a timer on your pity party. Set a timer, then go ahead and cry about not getting your dream job, dream account, much-deserved promotion, man or woman of your dreams, or whatever else you're mourning. When the timer goes off, you're done feeling sorry for yourself. Wipe your eyes, put a smile on your face, walk out the door, and start working on your next proposal.

An executive in one of my women's leadership courses shared how she used this with her daughter. When her daughter calls to complain, whine, or moan about some life event—when my daughters were growing up I used to call it the crisis du jour—this mother would put a timer on for five minutes and explain that the daughter has five minutes to complain, whine, moan, and lament that the world is not fair. When the timer goes off–ding! —the mother changes the conversation to another topic. Brilliant. I wish I had known about this strategy when my daughters were younger. However, I can attest it works well with children, and students, of any age.

CONFIDE IN A FRIEND

This is a fairly easy resilience strategy that I like and use frequently, and yet, I find the women I coach, especially younger women, using it less and less. Throughout my eight years of leading women in the practice of resilience, I observe women confiding in a friend (another woman) less frequently than ever. When I first started experimenting with teaching women how to fail or, in more positive terms, how to become resilient after failing, "Confide in a friend" was a commonly used strategy. However, within the last couple of years, the "Confide in a friend" strategy is used so infrequently I have to actively promote it and beg women to try it. I haven't yet had to offer bribes, but the fact that I might have to add an incentive to encourage women to confide in each other gives me pause. More on women supporting women later.

When explaining this strategy—one that I employ on a regular basis—I ask women to explain why it isn't used as frequently as it was in the past. The answer is always the same: social media. We're in an age of social media where every post about every person and event can be doctored and adjusted to make everyone and everything look perfect. No wonder we are so afraid of making a mistake, much less admitting a mistake. My plea to get off social media falls on deaf ears as I expect, but I make the request anyway. At the very least, I implore women to reread the section on perfectionism.

I think there is another, sadder reason why we are more hesitant to confide in a friend. Thanks to the COVID-19 pandemic and social restrictions employed to keep it at bay, I have seen a marked downturn in social skills. Even seasoned sales professionals who can sell ice cream to snowmen admit they are struggling to get comfortable again with face-to-face communication and relationships. And these are people who make their livelihood being able to walk up to a stranger, start a conversation, build a relationship, and not rely on alcohol for courage. Post-COVID, I find myself spending more time than ever helping employees learn to start a conversation with a stranger, find commonality, ask questions, and be curious when talking with people. My concern is that we are confiding in friends less frequently than before is because we don't have friends to confide in. As highlighted in the

Women Supporting Women section of this guidebook, we were never designed to do life alone. Intentionally seeking out friends with whom you can share the good, the bad, and the ugly, is important and is an affirmative resilience strategy.

What does this strategy involve? As the name suggests, instead of hiding the failure deep inside of you where it festers and grows—oftentimes to massive proportions—you open up to a friend, become vulnerable, and share your mishap and subsequent feelings of failure. Vulnerability sounds easy enough but, in reality, it can conjure up scary thoughts. What will they think of me? Will they judge me? Will they not like me anymore? And the list of social fears goes on and on. I used to fear being honest and vulnerable even with close friends because I was afraid that if they knew me, they wouldn't like me. Not true. And in fact, my ability to be vulnerable actually enhanced my close relationships and created deeper levels of trust.

However, there are a few caveats to be aware of when employing this strategy.

* First and foremost, choose your friend wisely. This person should be someone you trust. You don't want your failure ending up in someone else's Facebook post, so make sure this person is a dependable friend. It has been interesting to see who women choose to share their failures with. Women tend to share with other women or their mother. In contrast, my observation supported by research suggests that men use this strategy even less than the women do and, when they use it, they share their failure with women. While my sample with men is much smaller than the number of women I work with, I still find it interesting that I have yet to personally learn of a man confiding in another man. I'm not saying it's not out

there. But I don't hear about men confiding in other men like women confiding in women. Maybe this is something that needs to change and a place where women can help.

* In addition to choosing your friends wisely, I also suggest a second layer of protective confidentiality. When sharing a failure, I always ask the friend to keep it confidential. I know, you would assume your friend would automatically understand that you wouldn't want this embarrassing information to be passed around like the children's game of telephone. But it is dangerous and foolhardy to assume that everyone thinks like us. Even my dear sweet husband, who would never do anything intentionally to hurt me, needs to be reminded to "Please keep this confidential." In my experience, whenever I explicitly ask for confidentiality—see the Ask for What You Want section—I get it. When I assume confidentiality, it has gone both ways. Don't take a chance and instead ask that your friend keep the conversation in confidence. And if she doesn't? She's not a friend and now you know.

* The other thing to remember is that good friends are not unbiased. Thank goodness! I wouldn't want it any other way. In many cases, I don't want a friend who tells me the truth: "Yes Jane, you are correct. You made a fool out of yourself and now everyone thinks you're an idiot." I want a friend who understands and empathizes with my embarrassment and fear and realizes that even if the previous statement was true, articulating it is not helpful. When confiding in a friend, you want to lean on a friend that supports you. True—in some cases that means telling you a hard truth, but not in this case. You're looking for emotional support, not deep-cutting feedback.

Reflect—Has anyone ever shared a failure with you? How did you react? My guess is that you were kind and sympathetic. Would you expect this friend to be the same way with you?

There are two positive outcomes that can emerge from the "Confide in a friend" strategy, which is why I encourage women to use it and men to try it. First, in every instance that I've been privy to, the confidant friend admitted to making the same failure at one time or another. That does not surprise me. As previously mentioned, after reading over 2,500 resilience papers, I have yet to see a failure that I have not also experienced. Yes, I am the Queen of Failure—but I honestly don't think I'm that exceptional when it comes to failing. The beauty of this strategy is that it makes everyone, the failer and the friend, aware that we are all in this together. We all make the same mistakes and feel bad about it. Instead of fearing that you are the only person who ever made that mistake, you learn that others have done the same thing—in many cases even worse—and you are not alone. There is great comfort in learning that you are not the only person who fails.

Secondly, when using this strategy, don't be surprised if you make a new friend. As crazy as it sounds, I've bonded with women over failure. We are relieved that we are not the only ones making mistakes and, in many cases, wind up laughing at ourselves instead of beating ourselves up. Confiding in a friend requires vulnerability and that vulnerability can become a source of strength and a new or stronger friendship.

And finally, there is also a benefit to getting the failure out of your head. For the same reason that I am a fan of journaling, talking a failure out with someone else will help you minimize its magnitude. It takes a lot of energy to be something you're not and, all too often, when hiding our failures out of fear, we spend way too much energy disguising, hiding, and burying our failures, or our perceived failures, so that no one will find out. Bringing a failure out in the open, to a carefully curated friend, gets the failure out of your head and into the light. And fear does not like light.

Remember, the best way to practice reframing failure and learn resilience is to write about them. Journaling is essential because it helps get the failure out of your head. This strategy takes that a step further. In addition to writing about your failure in your journal, you talk about it to a trusted friend. The effect is the same. It's no longer rattling around in your head.

A truly good friend allows you to vent your frustration and can give you brutal honesty but is always kind and comforting. Make sure you choose your friends wisely. You might also be surprised to learn that your friend has encountered this failure as well.

Practice—Next time you screw up, take a deep breath and share that mishap with someone you trust. What happened? How did you feel after sharing?

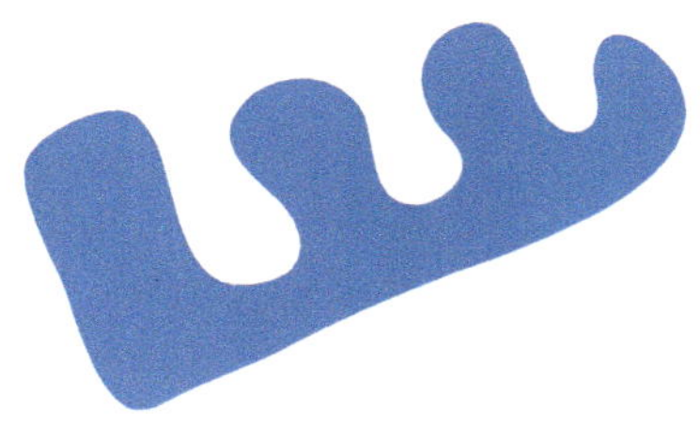

Practice—Next time you screw up, take a deep breath and share that mishap with someone you trust. What happened? How did you feel after sharing?

BE PATIENT

Full disclosure: This is a resilience strategy that I do not like nor do I like to use it. For the record, I am not a patient person. I was born in the fast-food generation. I want it now, thank you very much. And if I don't get it now, I get discouraged, downtrodden, and depressed. Seriously. I am not good at waiting. And I don't do it patiently. But I also recognize that in many cases, the situation is out of our control. Really?!? Control again??? But I like to think I'm in control of everything!!! That's right, sometimes we do our best, but there are other factors we can't control. There is no alternative but to be patient. Ugh.

Friendly reminder, what happens when we fail? If it's me, I automatically jump to the conclusion that it's my fault and I've done something wrong. And that may be true. But it may also be true that the failure really had nothing to do with me and my abilities. It is possible there were circumstances beyond my control (ugh–control again) that influenced the outcome I was so heavily invested in. In these cases, patience is the best strategy.

In 1995, I completed my doctoral dissertation on women and relationship selling—the primary sales tactic used in business-to-business sales at that time. The premise of my work was that if corporations wanted to build relationships with their customers to increase sales, they needed to look at hiring women. I proposed the idea that women were naturals at building relationships and would be excellent salespeople. Keep in mind, this was 1995. At that time, there were virtually no women in outside sales. Just ten years earlier, I wrote in my MBA notes that women cannot be in sales because they can't travel. Don't ask me to explain that one. I just wrote down what I was taught.

As you might guess, my dissertation research went absolutely nowhere. Nada. I barely got one publication from the data. No one was interested in hearing that women might be different from men and have unique skills that would benefit them in top sales positions. At that time, equal meant the same and my research suggested that women might have an advantage in certain situations. I was told by journal editors and sales executives—all men, I might add—that I couldn't say that maybe, just maybe, women had innate skills that might make them especially good at relationship sales—because men and women were the same. It was unfair to say that women might have an advantage over men in some aspects of selling. Grateful I didn't get burned at the stake for heresy, I gave up on researching women and sales, and instead turned to topics with a greater chance of getting published and getting tenure.

Fast forward to 2023 where businesses are desperately trying to diversify their sales force, especially in terms of hiring women. All the sudden, my research and focus on the unique set of skills that women bring to the sales process are in high demand. The insights that I discovered years ago when researching my dissertation, instead of being ignored, are now valued. Corporations seek my advice and pursue my women in sales students for lucrative sales positions.

What changed? Circumstances beyond my control. My passion for getting women into upwardly mobile, predominately male, industries like B2B sales has not changed. But society has changed and, **thirty** years later, my work is finally getting recognition.

Women find a patience strategy especially useful when applying for jobs. As we all know, landing a job is serious business. In addition to a job, we also pursue people we want to work with, projects we want to work on and opportunities we want to explore. We get interviews and call backs and are sure we got the job, the promotion, the project. And sometimes we do. But sometimes we don't, and in many cases, a reason for the rejection is not offered.

Like most of us, the first thing the women I coach assume is that they're not good enough or they did something wrong. And after talking with them, role playing the request, and reviewing their qualifications, in some rare cases, that is true. The failure was their fault, they fix their mistake, and they go back and apply again. But in most cases, the rejection has nothing to do with them and their abilities. There are a multitude of factors that come into play—especially after final interviews have taken place—and most of them are out of the applicant's control. But the hurt and disappointment of not receiving the promotion, the project, or the opportunity you thought was eminent, is painful. Even if you can rationalize that it wasn't "a fit," it still hurts.

In one instance, a woman told me about her job search process at her dream company. She met the company recruiters at a career fair, aced a telephone interview and was flown to company headquarters for the final round of interviews. She thought the job was hers. She did well in the final interviews and assumed an offer was forthcoming. But the offer never came. And when the rejection letter finally arrived weeks later, she was heartbroken and started blaming herself and beating herself up for not being good enough.

Thank goodness she remembered this strategy. The reality is that she had no idea why she didn't receive the offer. It could be that the position funding was pulled, there was a hiring freeze, or the president's nephew applied for the job. In fact, there are any number of reasons why, after a good interview, a job offer didn't materialize. In this case, she decided to be patient. She knew her resume was solid and that she interviewed well. She had confidence that if she was patient and kept applying for jobs, she would eventually get an offer. And she did. And it was an even better opportunity than the one that rejected her.

The key to staying patient is remaining active while waiting. Once again, I am not a patient person, so as my father would say, "Don't do as I do, do as I say" but even for someone as impatient as me, staying active while waiting helps. Girlfriend, I have wasted way too many hours waiting for the phone for ring with the man—or in the case of junior high, boy—of my dreams to call. Enough waiting. Stay active while you wait patiently.

While I love hearing women report their excitement about a promising job interview and a potential offer in process, I remind them to send thank you notes and keep applying for jobs. Keep yourself busy while you wait. While waiting for people to understand the value of my work on women in sales, I kept busy researching other areas. While you're waiting for a job offer, promotion, or other opportunity, stay busy applying for other openings.

Perhaps, even if you did everything right, it just wasn't the right time. Your prediction was accurate, but your colleagues were slow to see your vision. The interview went great, but HR is taking its time processing the approval. Sometimes you must wait patiently for the outcome, confident that you did what you could.

Practice—I hate to recommend this, because, as we already know, I have a hard time being patient. But is there a time when you failed and needed to practice patience while waiting for the next opportunity? Did things eventually work out? My guess is it did, and my guess is that it wasn't as quick as you would have liked it. But it eventually worked out.

KNOW WHEN TO QUIT

Unlike persistence, where the idea is that you keep going no matter what, there are occasionally times when the healthiest thing to do is quit. That's right. I said it. Quit. The whole idea of quitting gets a bad rap in our culture. Is there anything worse than being called a quitter? The term seems to conjure up images of a loser, someone weak in character, who doesn't have the guts to complete whatever it is they are doing.

Interesting, our connotation of quitting is quite different from the original meaning of the word which accounts for our hesitancy to do it. Turns out, the origin of the word "quit" comes from the root word "quieteth" which means to set ourselves free. Let that meaning soak in a bit—to "quit" something originally meant to set ourselves free. Wow. I did not see that one coming. Quitting used to be associated with something beautiful and liberating. What a lovely thought.

Reflecting back on the times I have used this strategy and "knew when to quit," it did, in fact, set me free, but that is not what it felt like at the time. And I cannot count the number of women I've had in my office who knew in their hearts, they need to quit something—a job, a friendship that is no longer a friendship, an organization, a church, a spouse—and yet, trudge on in the toxicity because they were told to never quit.

With such a beautiful denotation, how did the concept of quitting become such a demeaning term? According to research the term was manipulated by wealthy business owners during the industrial revolution. They needed factory workers to be productive and work ceaselessly regardless of the low pay and horrendous work conditions. To keep people working and producing, the industrialists shamed individuals who did not conform to their neck-breaking, soul-sucking productivity demands. The industrialists suggested quitting reflected weak moral character. Real men (and women) don't quit. And here we are today.

I agree that never giving up does have its place in life. Where would we be today without Winston Churchill's "Never ever, ever give in" speech? We'd all be speaking German. I have nothing against persistence. I am a fan of Angela Duckworth's GRIT research that demonstrates the power of stick-to-it-ive-ness. However, I have also seen and experienced times when quitting truly "set me free" and allowed other, better, opportunities to appear that would not have been possible had I insisted on being persistent. The tricky part—that I don't have a good answer for—is knowing when to quit and when to persist.

Warning—this strategy is to be used extremely judiciously and infrequently. In the course of my long life, I've used it twice. Observing women who have used it—it is once again used rarely and judiciously. Knowing when to quit doesn't mean that when life gets hard, you throw in the towel and call it a day. No. In fact, if you're thinking about quitting because things are hard, you probably need to learn persistence.

Knowing when to quit involves having the courage to recognize and respond to a toxic situation or individual that is draining your soul and energy. Fortunately, most of us do not encounter toxic situations or people on a regular basis. Thank goodness. But when you are entrapped in a toxic situation, persistence will only serve to dig your pit deeper; you need to quit and move on with your life.

As I stated earlier, I've only used this strategy occasionally—not to say I haven't quit jobs, relationships, clubs because they weren't what I wanted—but only twice that I can recall have I opted out of a toxic situation that, once relieved of the burden, my life blossomed in a different direction. In both cases, had I not quit, the new opportunity would not have been available to me. But make no mistake, quitting is hard because you have invested time and energy into the situation and subsequently, experience loss when you quit.

The personal example I share concerns an article a friend and I worked on for ten—yes, count them, ten years—in an attempt to get it published. We started working on this paper when we were doctoral students together. With each round of submissions and revisions, we collected new data, we analyzed the data, we added new citations, we wrote and rewrote the manuscript. We submitted to various editors and received more "revise and resubmit" responses than I can count. In some cases, we revised and resubmitted and received another "revise and resubmit" review.

This went on for ten years and we both became obsessed with seeing this article in print. I would fantasize how I would proclaim to my colleagues that my work had been published and we would celebrate the accomplishment together. I imagined where my husband would take me for dinner and how I would explain to my daughters, in simple terms, the magnitude of this accomplishment.

Only it was not to be. After investing ten years of our time, scouring thousands of data entries, and rewriting the article at least 20 times, my friend and I began to think of this paper as the albatross around our necks. We believed in our work and devoted untold amounts of cognitive and emotional energy to seeing it in print. Yet with ten years of work behind us, we had nothing to show for our trouble. At the end of ten years, we both separately came to the same conclusion. As painful as it was, we realized that this project was sucking us dry, and preventing us from pursuing other, more rewarding opportunities. We knew it was time to quit.

In this case, quitting was hard. We had both individually, and collectively, invested so much time and energy into seeing this project succeed. It was hard to watch ten years of work go down the drain with nothing, absolutely nothing, to show for our efforts. Yet, we both knew we could not continue to work on this article. It was time to quit.

Here's the funny thing about quitting. As painful as it was to admit defeat and the loss of ten years' worth of work, quitting work on that project was the best thing that happened to both of us. Once free from underneath the pressure to publish that work, we both turned to different research directions. She reinvigorated her work on customer satisfaction, and I returned to my work on women in business-to-business sales. And we both were far more successful in those respective areas than we were while engaged in our original research project. Had I not let go and quit researching consumer affect (the topic of the paper), I never would have had the time, energy, or opportunity to work on women in sales, which has formed the basis of my academic and professional career. And my friend would say the same. But we had to quit, before we could see the better opportunity.

While I warn women to use this resilience strategy sparingly, and they comply, there are two notable examples of its use that remain etched in my memory. In the first instance, a woman was in a toxic relationship with a young man. He was demeaning to her and disrespectful. She categorized the relationship as toxic. Yet they had been together for a significant amount of time, she was invested in the relationship, and she was hesitant to end it because she held out hope that he would change and they could live happily ever after. Nonetheless, even though scared, she used the "know when to quit" strategy and ended the relationship. At the end of the year, she wrote to tell me it was the best thing she ever did. She focused on her work and healing the wounds of the toxic relationship. Last I heard, she was pursuing her dream career in New York City.

The second example that sticks in my memory is of a woman who worked for a manager that treated her poorly, berated her for things that weren't her fault, and scheduled her to work on days she requested off. Nonetheless, they kept dangling the promise of a promotion in front of her. As bad as things were, she continued to hold out for that promotion and pay raise. Finally, after being chastised yet again for something beyond her control, she determined it was a toxic situation that was draining her emotionally, physically, and spiritually. Even though she needed the money from the job, she knew it was time to quit. And she did. To her surprise and joy, she applied for three jobs the following day, received two offers, and is now making more money and working for a supervisor who respects her and treats her well. But she would never have found the second job if she hadn't quit the other one first.

How do you know when it's time to quit? I wish I had an easy answer. Have I quit in situations I probably should have persevered? Sure. Have I stayed too long in situations where I should have quit? Absolutely. The hardest thing about this strategy is knowing when to use it. The other thing that makes it hard to know when to quit is that, in all of the cases I cite, hope is what kept us all in these toxic situations. We all kept plugging away in the toxic swamp because we all hoped things would change without us having to take scary action steps. In my case, my friend and I continued to hope that some editor would finally recognize the brilliance of our work and accept it for publication. In the case of my friends, they held out hope that the boyfriend or the boss would change. In all cases, we eventually recognized it was time to quit.

That which you can tolerate, you will not change.

While you won't use this strategy often, remember that sometimes it makes sense to acknowledge defeat and move on. By admitting that, you can change direction and be successful on a different path.

Practice—*Take inventory and see if there are any toxic situations, committees, projects, relationships, friendships, etc. where you need to quit. After the initial fear, was it the right thing to do? My guide? Good decisions bring peace.*

PART 3

CONFIDENTLY COMMUNICATE COMPETENCE—

DON'T GIVE YOUR POWER AWAY

"The most common way people give up their power is by thinking they don't have any." —Alice Walker

Here is a statistic that gave me pause. According to research, credibility is:

- 58% body language
- 35% tone or how you say it
- 7% what you say.

Let these numbers sink in a bit. According to this research, 93% of being perceived as credible is based upon your body language and how you say it, not how much you know. Ouch. This hurts for someone like me who has spent a lifetime in college—first an undergraduate degree, then an MBA followed by a PhD. That's over nine years of college. And now you're telling me that it doesn't matter how much I know—I will not be perceived as being credible if I don't use credible body language and speaking tone??? The sad reality—and I've seen it in action—is yes. Credibility is not dependent upon what you know; it's how you communicate it.

Every time I look at those numbers, it takes my breath away. First off, what do we mean by credibility? I see credibility as a first cousin, or maybe even sibling, to confidence. A credible speaker is someone who knows what they're talking about—i.e., they have confidence in what they are saying. Credibility is knowing your stuff and making it clear that you know what you're talking about. Why do I keep hammering this point home? Because in my experience, many women know what they are talking about. They have the knowledge, the research and/or the experience to support what they are saying. But you'd never guess it from the way they were communicating. They sound unsure of themselves; they appear to be unsure of themselves (a.k.a. lack confidence) with the result making it appear they have only marginal knowledge.

As a college professor and business consultant, I have had a front row seat to observe actual knowledge—as reflected in a grades and job performance reviews—versus the way women and men convey that knowledge. It was soul crushing for me to watch the best and brightest women consistently sell themselves short when it came to self-evaluation. The women knew the material. They knew the product. They knew what objections to expect. I knew from practicing with them in preparation for big meetings that they knew their stuff. They were competent. Yet these accomplished women would go into a corporate meeting or sales presentation and become wimps.

In contrast, I would watch the men, bless their hearts, brag outside the meeting room, about how easy this was going to be. They didn't need to prepare. You just do it. And of course, they sounded great—they just had no idea about the customer, the product they were selling, or other relevant details.

I had one young man speak with such confidence, he almost had me convinced that the 3rd party logistics company he was selling owned their own fleet of trucks. In case you're wondering, the fact that the company is in 3rd party logistics means they do not own their own truck fleet; instead, they subcontract with independent truckers to broker shipments. This man almost convinced me that that he knew what he was talking about. But he had no clue. Conversely, the women knew the material, but were scared to death to let their knowledge show.

This statistic—credibility is 58% body language, 35% how you say it, and a mere 7% what you say—explained my pain. The women knew what to say—but unfortunately knowing what to say is only a small fraction of how we communicate credibility. The man in the extreme example above (and let me be clear—there are competent men) had minimal expert knowledge, but he knew how to convey credibility through his body language and how they spoke. Ouch. And I have fallen into the same trap. I knew what I was talking about but was afraid to show it. And without strong body language and tone, all the knowledge in the world gets overlooked as not credible.

On the positive side, these numbers give hope for an introvert like me. The thing that warms my heart about this statistic is that I can convey confidence without even opening my mouth. 58% of credibility is conveyed through body language, and I can do that without talking. Whew. For introverts like me, this takes the weight of the world off my shoulders. It means I can demonstrate credibility—that I know my stuff—without saying a word. What a relief. Talk about taking the pressure off. And believe me, I've learned powerful body language, and you can too.

Side note. *Even though I appear to be outgoing, my worst nightmare is when my husband, the resident extrovert, comes home with a party invitation. A little background here—my husband is the kind of guy who makes friends with everyone. And if he isn't your friend, he just hasn't met you yet, but he will. As you might guess, he frequently comes home with party invitations. My first response is "Do I have to go?" As introverts will attest, how else would you respond to a party invitation? If the invitation has political overtones as part of his administrative position, and declining is not an option, my second question is "How long do we have to stay?" We haven't even arrived at the gathering and I'm already looking forward to going home. My main criterion for choosing purses is that they are large enough to hold my Kindle. Never attend a party without something to read. So, when I claim to be an introvert I know what I'm talking about. For an insightful and feel-good analysis of introversion, read* Quiet *by Susan Cain.*

Because body language is processed at a subconscious level, no one ever thinks to criticize body language. Have you ever been in a conversation where someone whispered, "Wow. Did you see Mary's body language? She was looking pretty strong and powerful." Probably not. But we've all been in conversations where a woman has been criticized for talking in an aggressive or assertive tone of voice. The complaint that "who does she think she is—talking like that?" is likely accompanied by the B-word.

Yes. I know—there is a double standard. Men use a strong and powerful tone of voice and they're praised for being assertive; women use the same tone and we're criticized for being a B----. As noted multiple times throughout this book, you and I cannot change the world—at least not today—but we can change the way we communicate. And by learning to use strong and powerful body language and tone, we can increase our credibility without threatening others.

In this part, we're going to break apart confident communication into three topic areas—writing, speaking, and body language. We'll start with writing because, as an undergraduate English major, writing is the easiest one to change. Consider how much communication takes place via emails. In many cases, your first introduction to a potential client, co-worker, or boss, will be via email so it's important to get it right the first time. The other reason I like working with emails is because they are the easiest medium to notice and correct mistakes. I virtually never send an email in its initial form. I read it, correct it—in most cases, multiple times—and then send it.

Next, we'll center our discussion on talking. It's harder to change self-limiting speech habits because, face it, we're thinking about what to say (7% of credibility), not how to say it (35% of credibility). And if you're like me, I say it, and then realize I've made a mistake. But it's easy to listen to the speech of others and notice when they undermine their power. Knowledge is power and studying the less than stellar speech habits of other unconfident women, helps you identify your own issues. Once you're made aware of power-draining speech habits, you can practice replacing them with strong, self-affirming language.

Then we'll focus on the most significant aspect of credibility: body language. Body language is so powerful (friendly reminder—over half of credibility is communicated without saying a word) that little changes in body language can mean a lot. But I'll be honest. Body language is hard to change. Why? Because most of us are not looking at ourselves while we're talking, negotiating, or giving a presentation. I have joked with many a company about fitting a room with full length mirrors. If I had mirrors, and women could watch themselves as they habitually make themselves small when talking, presenting, and selling, the problem would be corrected. Give me mirrors instead of technology. As you've probably guessed, my plea goes unheeded. But good news: With the ease of video recording, watching yourself is easier than ever. Equally painful, but at least it's easy to video record.

We'll conclude this section with topics related to communication—accepting compliments (spoiler alert—we don't do it well), handling interruptions (we don't do that well either), and refusal skills or learning how to say no (a critical skill for survival if you're a people-pleaser). Let's get started.

POWER WRITING—
TRIM THE HEDGES WHEN YOU WRITE
(AND I'M NOT TALKING ABOUT LANDSCAPING)

CONFIDENTLY COMMUNICATE CONFIDENCE— DON'T GIVE AWAY YOUR POWER

"Clear is kind."~—Brené Brown

Why are we talking about writing first? Because it's the easiest to correct. As an undergraduate English major, I learned the value of writing, re-writing, and in many cases, re-writing yet again. Case in point, while writing and re-writing the manuscript for this book, my beloved editor would eventually become exasperated with my re-writes (perfectionism rearing its ugly head yet again?) and declare enough. It is written. Stop re-writing.

The value of writing is that you have a chance to get your ideas on paper, or on the computer screen first, (the 7% what you say of credibility), then edit how you say it which is almost three times (35%) more important. And writing is especially important when it comes to emails because of the speed of delivery. A personal favorite mantra is "respond—don't react" and truer words have never been spoken when dealing with emails. A reaction email is a snotty-gram where, what you say may be true, but the way you say it will send negative reverberations forever. A respond email takes time to think about how to say it so that the message is more likely to be acknowledged.

POWER WRITING—EMAILS: LESS IS MORE

So, let's back up a minute. Think about how you read your emails. Where are you, and what device—laptop or phone—do you use to read your emails? Sometimes we may use our laptops, but in many cases, we read emails on our phones. Now think about the issue with that. Consider the size of an average phone screen. A grammatically correct, well-composed, lengthy sentence reads well on a laptop screen. That same sentence when read on a phone, makes the sentence look like the preface to a Russian novel (friendly reminder—*Anna Karenina* by Tolstoy is over 1,400 pages in print).

Now take this a step further. What do you do when an email is too long? Tell the truth. If you're like me, I delete it. I'm not going to read all that text on a phone screen. At best, I might skim a long email. But most likely, I delete it. Unread. Game over.

Why am I spending so much time trying to convince you to shorten your emails? Because it's hard. And we are not in the habit of doing it. The quickest and easiest way to shorten emails and make a bigger statement, is to cut out the filler words. Time to start trimming.

Try this little experiment. These are excerpts from real emails from real women. I'm not making this up. Keep in mind, I love helping the women I mentor uncover their power and will do anything within my power to help them. So, a woman I'm working with makes a request of me, she is likely to get it, because I love helping people, especially my mentees. Yet look at this writing. I'm only giving you the excerpt; the actual email took up half a page (or at least it seemed that way). And this is from a well-respected woman manager.

> Dear Dr. Sojka
>
> ...I was wondering if you would be willing to help us promote our activity. We would like to ask if you could possibly please share this information with your colleagues....

Practice—*Take out the filler words in the previous two sentences. What is the fewest number of words that you can use to make your request?*

When I first introduced this activity, I was dumbfounded by the results. Women were OK about eliminating some of the extra words, but it was the men who nailed the assignment. What did the men write? For the first sentence, "Would you promote our activity?" And the second sentence? "Please share this information. . . ." The men (and to be clear, these are not the brightest nor best performers) instinctively reduced a 14-word sentence to five words. And the men's second sentence was just as brief.

Research confirms what I've observed; women tend to add more filler words, hedges, and intensifiers than men. Furthermore, because as women, we're used to padding requests with filler words, we expect everyone to write that way. Consequently, we can misinterpret email messages that are short and to the point as unfriendly or animosity.

As part of my faculty appointment, I served on our university Institutional Review Board where all research that involved human subjects—that means people in scientific terms—was reviewed to confirm the experiment participants were safe and respected and that no federal, state, or local regulations were violated. The members on this committee were scientists and medical doctors.

When I had questions or concerns about a particular piece of research, I would spend hours writing long, glorious emails to the IRB head, explaining my position and concerns. To my dismay, I would receive a short, two sentence response. I assumed he hated me. Why else would he not respond at length? Once I started studying gender differences—and in this case, probably academic discipline differences too—in communication, his stark emails made sense. It had nothing to do with me. He was efficient and to the point. And patterning my responses to his style greatly helped our communication.

Reflect—*Why do we add so many filler words to our emails?*

When I read the "I was just wondering if you would be willing to help us . . ." out loud, the groveling tone of request is unavoidable. It is as if we are afraid to ask "would you . . ." so instead, we grovel and plead and hope that the reader will consider our pathetic plea for help.

Whoa! Wait a minute. Remember, I told you this email came from a woman—a sharp conscientious woman—and as her mentor, I'm inclined to go out of my way to help her. So why is she groveling?

My guess, reinforced by women I work with, is that we are afraid to ask for what we want. We hope that by adding enough filler words, we sound humble and polite. The reality is that we sound small and pathetic. Seriously. What's the worst that can happen? The reader, in this case me, might say no. So what? Move on to the next person. Instead of asking for what we want, we make ourselves small and pitiable. Remember—you can be pitiful or powerful, but you can't be both. Pick one. And there's no question which one I pick. There are enough people out there who want to make us small—so why would we want to do it to ourselves?

Instead of using fluffy language, there are other ways to convey care and concern for the addressee. I like to start an email with something personal that shows I care about the individual. It could be something as simple as "I hope you had a good weekend . . ." But if I know someone has been sick, or a family member is sick, I'll start the email with "How is your dad doing? I hope he's doing OK." Or you can close the message with a note of appreciation such as "Thanks again for all you do to make this a positive experience for our new team members." Adding a personal sentence conveys your care and concern for the other person without diminishing your power.

CUT THE HEDGES
(AND I DON'T MEAN TRIM THE SHRUBS)

There are other ways we weaken ourselves and give away our power when we write. How often do you use these words in your writing?

* I think
* I feel
* Maybe
* Perhaps
* Kind of
* Almost

The bottom line for all of these words or phrases is that they convey weakness, insecurity, and a lack of confidence.

These words are considered hedges—it is as if we're afraid to definitively state our position and instead, soften our language when we're uncomfortable asserting our ideas or afraid of being perceived as too aggressive. All of these undermining speech habits give away power. Which sounds more compelling?

"I think the thing to do is…"   Or "the thing to do is…"

Taking out the hedges or fillers doesn't make you sound aggressive; instead, you sound competent and confident. And here's the other thing. We think we're making ourselves more likable by using soft language but the reality is that if someone wants to attack you for your ideas or for who you are, they will come after you no matter how much you try to soften your language. You might as well say what you need to say and eliminate the hedges. But wait, there's more.…

OTHER WORDS TO AVOID IN EMAILS:

Just

How many times have you started an email with "I'm *just* checking in.…" Until I made a conscious decision to stop giving away my power, the word "just" appeared throughout my messages. Think of what you're really communicating when you insert the word "just" in your communication. We use "just'" when we feel we need to apologize, or when we're worried about coming on too strong. It's as if we're saying, "I *only* want to say.…" Really?!? Don't apologize. Say it.

Listen to the difference in these phrases—

* "I'm *just* checking in …" versus "I'm checking in …"
* "I'm *just* concerned that …" versus "I'm concerned that …"

—*What does each version say about the speaker? Which speaker would you rather hire or work with?*

Actually

While I'm more of a "just" girl, and I must continually practice eliminating the word "just" from my writing and speaking, one of my daughters actually has the same issue with the word, you guessed it, "actually." Typical talk would include "I *actually* think . . ." Or "I *actually* disagree . . ." Think about what you're actually saying when you overuse the word "*actually.*" It is as if you're surprised you have a thought or that you disagree. Figure out your filler of choice and practice eliminating it.

OTHER WEAK WORDS TO AVOID—INTENSIFIERS

Intensifiers have the same de-valuing effect on writing as hedges. An intensifier is an added word that increases the magnitude of statement. Intensifiers include words like **so**, **very**, **always**, **never**, **only**, **quite**, etc. Instead of saying "I'm happy to help" we add "I'm always happy to help" thus intensifying our commitment to oblige instead of being direct: happy to help. When we write, "I'm *very* excited" . . . instead of "I'm excited" we think we are increasing the magnitude of our enthusiasm, but in reality, we're over exaggerating because we don't think our excitement (without the very) is enough. It is. Cut out the intensifiers.

How ingrained are these writing habits? Old habits die hard. In the course of writing the manuscript for this book, I cannot tell you how many times I inserted the word "so" in a sentence. (And truth be told, my editor wanted to slash even more.) It is as if I have to intensify what I'm trying to say in order to get the reader to listen. Not true. Many of the "so" words originally in this manuscript have fortunately hit the cutting room floor.

WATCH THE !!!!!

And as long as we're talking about language that undermines our power, let's not forget the overuse of exclamation points and, my personal favorite, the smile. Context is everything and if you're writing to your mother or best friend, your style will be different from an email written to your boss or company CEO. I confess, I tend to include smiley faces when writing emails to people I care about—my daughters, family members, mentees, close girlfriends. I truly (note the use of an intensifier) want these special people to know I care about them and that I'm warm and friendly—not cold and aloof. So, I use smiley faces to convey my friendlessness and willingness to help.

But if I'm writing to in a professional context—even if I know the person semi-well, the exclamation points and smiley faces are a no-go. I convey warmth by an introductory sentence and keep the writing short and to the point. I remove the hedges, intensifiers, and exclamation points before sending.

Practice—Which of these undermining speech habit traps are you most likely to fall into? Pick the one that you want to eliminate and proofread every email to eliminate it before sending. If you're still concerned that you might sound too bold without the hedges or fillers, ask a friend to read the email and see if it sounds pushy. I've done this many times for mentees and women I coach and have yet to read a powerfully written email that offends me. On the contrary, the writing sounds confident and professional and the direct approach is appreciated.

 I'm serious about picking only one habit to work on. If you try to eliminate all your bad writing habits, you'll feel overwhelmed and defeated. Small changes can yield a big impact. I'm a big on starting small. Pick one area you want to improve and focus on that. After you've changed your habit, then move to another focus. And remember, the operative word is practice. Do I still catch myself inserting "just" in a sentence? You betcha. But I forgive myself—failure is an event, not a person—and move on knowing that I'll catch it the next time. Small changes bring big results.

Do you have someone who would pre-read your emails and give you honest feedback? I offer this service to all my mentees and many take me up on it. They craft their email, eliminate the hedges and qualifiers and then send it to me for a second opinion. Their initial fear is that the email sounds too harsh.

Their fear is unfounded. In my ten years of pre-reading powerfully revised emails from mentees, I have yet to read one that offended me with its abruptness. In fact, I read the email, subconsciously evaluated it as sounding professional (yay!!!) and then am shocked at the writer's "PS—did this sound pushy?" addendum. In virtually all cases, what initially feels pushy to the writer, comes across as professional to me. But my second reading, and confirmation, gives the woman the confidence to send the email and continue writing from a position of strength. Find someone who will do the same for you and be that reader for someone else.

Here's the thing about communication. We think the important part about communication is the message we send to the other person. And I agree. But it's also important to remember that we too are reading that message. And every time we use a hedge to undercut our authority or make ourselves small, we are communicating that message to ourselves. There are enough people who want to make us small and insignificant; we don't need to do it to ourselves. Stop it. Get comfortable with your power and don't give it away.

QUIT THE QUALIFIERS

CONFIDENTLY COMMUNICATING COMPETENCE

The previous section focused on writing. I like to start there when creating new habits because writing is easier to correct. Simply delete and replace. Speaking is harder for me since I tend to talk and then realize I could have said it better. Quick review—remember 37% percent of credibility is how you say it. Judging from the number of qualifiers I hear used by women (and men) in meetings, we need to some serious surgery on qualifiers and how to quit using them.

What's a qualifier? Qualifiers are phrases added to the beginning or end of a statement that undercut authority. Typical qualifiers are "I'm not an expert, but . . .", "I was just thinking . . .", "I just want to say," or, one of my personal favorites that I find annoying as heck, "Can I ask a question?" (after I've called on them because they had their hand up). When a woman asks permission to ask a question I want to scream—Yes! Yes! Ask your question. That's why I called on you. Ugh.

Sometimes qualifiers are used at the end of the sentence. I was in a meeting when a woman remarked that she completed a marathon last weekend, "but it wasn't a fast time because I was running with my friend who ran a slower pace." What?!?! Seriously?!?! You finished a marathon and then apologized because it wasn't as fast as normal? Think about the response you'd get if you asked a football player what position he plays. He'll tell you the position but will neglect to tell you he's never gotten in a game. And that's OK.

Reflect—Why do we start our brilliant comments with statements like "I'm not an expert but . . . , or "I just want to say . . ."?

There are a couple of reasons why we use qualifiers at the beginning of our brilliant statements. First—and yes, I know I've said this before but I'm saying it again—we're afraid we might be wrong. In fact, we're so afraid we might be wrong (i.e., fear of failure) that we factor failure into our otherwise intelligent statements. Starting a sentence with "I'm not an expert…" already accounts for the reason you might be wrong. Wait a minute. You haven't even made your statement and you're already figuring it might be wrong. Seriously?!?

A second reason why we add a qualifier before our dazzling statements is a false and inaccurate sense of humility. We are so afraid that we might offend someone by talking too bold, too proud, too assertive, that we undercut ourselves by watering our brilliance down. "I just wanted to say …" means shriveling, shrinking, cowering in the corner only wanting to get in a few words. Stop it. And stop it now.

You have a right to speak. And you have a right to make whatever statement you feel is appropriate. Now I'm not saying everyone will always agree with what you say. And if they don't? Who cares. You're resilient. You'll speak up again. But there is no need for you to diminish your presence to make others feel more comfortable.

THERE'S ONLY ONE THING TO DO WITH QUALIFIERS: ELIMINATE THEM

In department meetings, I used to start every sentence with "I'm not a researcher but," . . . and then make my statement. I'll admit, the first time I spoke up in a department meeting without using a qualifier, I was scared to death. To be clear, the men in my department had never made me feel anything less than equal. Yet I felt sure that without noting my shortcomings, the other faculty in the room would jump down my throat. I tried it anyway. I eliminated the qualifier, made my point, and guess what? Nothing happened. Absolutely nothing happened—except that I didn't give away my power. Cut the qualifiers.

Because most of us acquired the habit of using qualifiers, we need to consciously become aware of them so that we can eliminate their use. In some cases, other phrases can be substituted. Replace "I'm just thinking off the top of my head" with "let's do some brainstorming about this.…" Instead of concluding a statement with "does that make sense"? ask about them. "How did that land with you?" or "what are your thoughts?" My favorite way to break the qualifier habit is to say the qualifier silently to myself, then speak my statement out loud. Eventually, you'll forget the qualifier and go straight to the point. But it takes practice and attention.

I don't know about you, but I find it much easier to fix other people than work on my own stuff. Not good. But the first step in quitting qualifiers is becoming aware of them and how much you hear them. Once I started studying this stuff, I was appalled at how often I heard qualifiers—not just from students, but from top-ranking managers. It is a bad habit that we need to break. Here is the three-step process I've used to break the habit.

Step 1—Listen to how often you hear other women, and men, use qualifiers. Knowledge is power and once you become accustomed to hearing them in conversation, you'll recognize them in your speech as well.

Step 2—Knowing that I have a tendency to start a sentence with a qualifier, I mentally rehearse the statement before speaking it out loud, "I'm not an expert in this industry, but I wonder…" and note the qualifier. Then, I mentally whisper the qualifier to myself "I'm not an expert in this industry" and speak the statement "But I wonder. . . ." It feels awkward and tedious at first, but remember, these are habits ingrained in us over many years. It takes practice to undo the habit.

Step 3—Make a pact with a friend to privately (after the meeting) call each out when either one of you uses a qualifier. Stop the conversation, repeat the statement minus the qualifier. Ask your friend if you sounded pushy. Ask yourself if you felt you were being pushy. Guess what? You don't need qualifiers.

Practice—How do you build confidence? You practice. And quitting qualifiers is no exception. Notice how often you use them and use the three-step process to break the habit. Better yet, get a friend to help. If either of you uses a qualifier, gently point it out.

When a woman uses a qualifier in a workshop, I will call for a "redo" and have her repeat her brilliant statement minus the qualifier. Then I ask other women if she sounded pushy or arrogant. The answer is always no. I ask the woman if she felt pushy or arrogant without the qualifier. The answer again is always no. It's important to notice and validate that our fears of appearing too pushy or arrogant are unfounded. Instead, we sound competent and confident.

Do I still slip up and use qualifiers? Absolutely. But I'm getting better at eliminating them. Remember, when you communicate to others, you are also communicating to yourself. When you start a sentence with "I'm not an expert" both you and the receiver hear that message. When we use qualifiers, we weaken our authority and we hear ourselves as weak. Quit undermining your authority. You don't need to apologize for asking a question or not being an expert. Make your statement. Period. Don't give away your power. There are plenty of people who want to take our power; don't give it to them.

TALK LIKE AN EXPERT

USURP THE UPSPEAK

In addition to making wise word choice and quitting the qualifiers, speaking has additional components—speed, intensity, and pitch. While all play a role in sounding competent and credible, I'm going to focus on the one that trips other women and me up the most: pitch.

Have you watched reality TV lately? If so, you've probably been exposed to more upspeak than you care to acknowledge. Upspeak—where you end sentences by raising your vocal pitch instead of lowering it—is on its way to epidemic proportions in the United States. Credit the Kardashians or any number of other pop celebrities and you'll hear upspeak perfected. The problem is that no one takes an up-speaker seriously. They may be cool and hip in pop culture but they're not running for president, climbing a corporate ladder, or establishing expertise. Put politics aside and listen to Hillary Clinton, Nancy Pelosi, Kamala Harris or respected journalists like Nora O'Donnell, Leslie Stahl, and Savannah Guthrie (who is trained as a lawyer BTW). They speak slowly, lower their pitch when the sentence concludes, and pause between sentences. Wow. They sound powerful.

> *Reflect—Why do we soften our speech patterns by ending sentences with upspeak?*

Once again, (notice the pattern here) in our efforts to be likeable and friendly, we engage in upspeak. We are so desperate to come across as friendly and welcoming that we undercut our authority and sound like valley girls. Unfortunately, upspeak only serves to make us sound less authoritative and lacking confidence.

How difficult is it to break this habit? While coaching women to talk like an expert, I listened to my recorded message on my answering machine. How embarrassing. In my efforts to sound welcoming and friendly, I sounded like an idiot. It took me five times of re-recording to end each sentence with a period and pause. And guess what? I still sound friendly only now I sound professional as well.

Learning to talk like an expert takes practice. Remember, 37% of credibility is how you say it, not what you say—so you need not be the ultimate expert on the topic you're discussing.

You'll be amazed how convincing you can sound by varying your speech pattern. When I demonstrate this activity, after much practice, it is scary how competent I sound on a topic where I have only general information.

Now that you've practiced *talking* like an expert, let's practice *being* the expert.

The first time I did this exercise in a group, I was panicked. Petrified. Scared to death. No, I was not in first grade. I had my PhD, tenure, a thriving consulting business, and was respected in my field. And yet, I was terrified to claim expertise. When I practice this exercise with other women, I learn I am not alone.

There are numerous reasons why we are afraid to claim expertise, but none are legitimate and all can be handled gracefully with practice. A common fear is that someone else in the room also claims expertise in our area. So what? Who cares? Great. There can be more than one expert. Assuming that only one person can have the title expert in a given field is a mindset of scarcity and competition. If there can only be one, your focus will be on besting the other person and excluding them from the conversation so you can build yourself up.

In a scarcity and competition mindset, you need to be the expert, so you can win and they then lose. Not a positive environment. Here's the deal. Stop it. Now. Replace scarcity and competition with a mindset of abundance and cooperation. An atmosphere of cooperation and abundance stimulates the belief that there can be more than one expert and, in fact, you can learn and cooperate with each other to enhance the expertise of all. And remember, shining your light doesn't diminish the light of others; it makes the room brighter. So, shine on, sisters. Declare and share your expertise.

Another one of my biggest fears is not being able to live up to the expert title. What if someone calls you out—questioning your expertise or knowledge in the subject? First, let me share from personal experience exactly how many times that has happened to me. Zero. That's right, a big O. Nada. No way. Never. While we fear that people will call us out and we will be publicly shamed, that rarely happens. And if, or when it does, it says more about the person doing the name-calling than your expertise.

But if someone points out that you missed something or that you haven't read his/her latest book on the topic, it still isn't the end of the world. Do the same thing you do when someone brings a mistake to your attention: smile, say thank you, and ask for more information. "No, I haven't seen your study but I'd love to read it. Can you send it to me?" The heckler feels good because you acknowledged their expertise and you feel good because you didn't give away your power. Remember the words of Eleanor Roosevelt—*no one can make you feel bad about yourself without your permission.* I would add—don't give them permission.

> **Practice**—*How do you build confidence? Practice. Now go around the room or stand in front of a mirror and practice again saying "Hi, my name is ________________________, and I am an expert in __________________."*
>
> *Note: This is a practice exercise. Please do not go around introducing yourself as an expert. The purpose of this activity is to help you get comfortable accepting yourself as the expert you are.*

"You can always tell the strong women in the room—they're the ones building the others up."

SORRY, I'M NOT SORRY— ELIMINATING THE "S" WORD FROM YOUR VOCABULARY

STOP APOLOGIZING FOR THINGS THAT AREN'T YOUR FAULT: ELIMINATE SORRY

Imagine you're in a crowded hallway. What do you say when you accidentally bump into someone in a crowded space? My instinct, and since I was raised to be a nice girl, is to apologize and say "I'm sorry." Think about that for a minute. It is crowded hallway. I did not intentionally run into the other person. Nor did the other person intentionally (I'm assuming) run into me. Some architect designed the hallway too small and there is not enough space for all the people in it. So why am I apologizing? I have a right to be here. As does the other person. We have as much right to take up space as the other person. So why do we apologize for taking up space?

Reflect—Why do we apologize and say "sorry" so often?

Don't get me wrong, I appreciate manners and civility and believe kindness can go a long way in terms of healing misunderstandings. I would never want to behave in a rude or unkind way; nor would I ever teach my students to behave badly. But on the other hand, why should we apologize for things that are not our fault like accidentally running into someone in a crowded hallway? Research shows that women apologize more frequently than men. And apologizing for taking up space is only the beginning.

I've received emails from women apologizing for things that would break your heart. One woman apologized for having Multiple Sclerosis. Her email began, "Dr. Sojka, I'm so sorry for having to miss our class today. My MS has been acting up. . . ." Whoa! Hold up. You are a young woman dealing with a horrible disease and you're apologizing to me for missing a meeting? No way. Another equally disconcerting email arrived from a woman who almost lost her father in a car wreck. "Dear Dr. Sojka, I am sorry I have been so distant the last couple of weeks. My father was riding his bike when hit by a car and is currently in intensive care...." Oh my goodness. My heart sank. This young woman was dealing with her father's serious injuries and apologizing to me for not staying in touch?!? I think not. These are heartbreaking examples of where no apology is needed.

There are several reasons why we may overuse the word sorry. We want people to like us (attention all people-pleasers). We want to be nice. We don't want to cause trouble. And we certainly don't want to be perceived as pushy or rude or inconsiderate of others. So, yet again, we make ourselves small—by using qualifiers, hedges, small body language, and, in the case of "sorry," by apologizing for things that are not our fault. Are you beginning to see the theme here? In every form of communication, writing, talking, and being (body language) we make ourselves small to avoid the possibility that we may upset someone.

Turns out, I'm not the only woman who tends to make herself small by apologizing too frequently. Research reveals interesting gender differences in the use of apologies. In one of my favorite experiments, a professor gave every student a failing grade on an exam and then asked why did they fail. The explanations make me laugh to keep from crying. Turns out that when the women didn't do well, they attributed their failure to their own shortcomings—they weren't smart enough, they didn't deserve to be in the class, they didn't study enough, etc. The men? A different story. The men blamed their failure on the professor—not their own shortcomings. There is ample evidence to suggest that women are more likely to offer expressions of contrition than men. Yikes! No wonder apologizing has become a mainstay of our communication.

Needless to say, when I approach the topic of eliminating the word "sorry" in mixed gender situations, I have hesitations. On the one hand, there are men who need to apologize more. Even my devoted husband who brings me flowers and says nice things, rarely has the courage to mumble the s-word when he's messed up. But for women, and some men, it's a different story. I'm convinced that if you do something really wrong—you ran over my mother with your car—you need to apologize. But for most of us women, we need to practice apologizing less.

STOP APOLOGIZING FOR TAKING UP SPACE

Once I started studying, and consequently noticing, how frequently other women and I said "sorry" I knew this habit had to change. I also know, from putting into practice the many things I write about in this book, that old habits die hard. To eliminate "sorry" when accidentally bumping into people, I took a 3-step approach to breaking the habit.

Step 1—Notice the problem. I started noticing how often I said "sorry" and how often other women said it as well. Knowledge is power, and the first step to making changes is acknowledging the issue. And note, it is much easier, and much more fun, to notice how much other people mess up instead of acknowledging your own limitations. Enjoy it temporarily and then start looking at yourself.

Step 2—I wasn't ready to stop apologizing completely—remember, I'm still a nice girl—so I switched to "excuse me." This still sounded polite, but it was still an unnecessary apology. The "excuse me" was a nice middle step and I believe in being kind and considerate to others. However, the bottom line is that we have a right to take up space.

Step 3—After getting used to 'excuse me,' it was time to go all out and eliminate the apology altogether. Now, I use my secret weapon—my smile—and say, "no problem." The "no problem" makes it clear that the bump was an accident—no ill will towards anyone. And the smile is the non-verbal cue to communicate that I'm nice about it. It works. It conveys "I'm OK and you're OK" and we both go on our way. Do I still forget and revert back to my "sorry" when I inadvertently bump into someone? Absolutely. But with practice, I'm getting better at apologizing less.

Don't give away your power by apologizing for things that aren't your fault, such as the width of an overcrowded hallway.

REPLACE "SORRY" WITH "THANK YOU"

I like to keep things simple, so the easiest way I found to eliminate the word "sorry" is to replace it with "thank you." For example, think about what happens when you're unintentionally late. The traffic is bad, there's a wreck, you get a last-minute phone call that must be handled and voila! You're late. *(Note: If you are intentionally late—like my husband to church—this solution is not for you. You need to skip this section and go apologize].* Instead of apologizing for your tardiness—it's not your fault the road crews chose today to eliminate one lane of traffic—tell the waiting party, "Thank you for waiting for me."

Think about what you just said. First, you thanked them for waiting. Who doesn't like being thanked? It makes us feel good. Secondly, you didn't give away your power by groveling with the typical "I'm so sorry I'm late. I feel so bad that I made you wait…" Instead of apologizing, you thank them and make it clear you appreciate their time. And you're not giving away your power by being pitiful and begging for forgiveness for something that wasn't your fault. It's a win–win for all. And it works. I rarely use the word "sorry" now but am generous with giving others my gratitude and thanks.

A while back, I gave a workshop on cutting out apologies to women athletes, several of whom were on the same team. Word got back to me that they had eliminated the "sorry" on the field. Turns out, before learning about excessive apologies, every time a player made a mistake on the field, she would apologize to her teammates. "Sorry, bad pass." "Sorry I missed that." After my talk, the team decided to eliminate the word "sorry" when on the field and, instead, to keep playing. "Sorry" was not allowed. I wish I could say the team went on to become national champions. The reality is that I don't know how eliminating sorry affected their win–loss record. But I do know this. The women players felt stronger when they quit apologizing and making themselves small. Eliminating "sorry" from their vocabulary didn't hurt.

An added bonus for being frugal with apologies is that, when you quit saying sorry for things you can't control, your sympathy sounds more sincere when you truly are sorry. When someone I care about loses a family member or friend, I am truly sorry. I say it and I mean it. The overuse of sorry cheapens the emotion, and that is not our intention. Now I reserve "sorry" for meaningful occasions—such as death or a tragic loss—and I mean it.

And if you don't believe me about the power of eliminating "sorry," listen to a women's empowerment expert, Barbie, for a fun, but accurate, assessment on eliminating "sorry." This cartoon Barbie's Vlog captures our real–life behavior.

https://www.youtube.com/watch?v=g9ahiHpM3yQ

See how many of these situations you recognize.

I don't know about you, but I always find it easier, and face it, more ego-gratifying to observe other people's faults rather than work on my own. Ouch. However, there is value to observation. Knowledge is power, and once I started studying the debilitating nature of apologizing for things that aren't our fault I also started observing how often I heard women, and some men, continually saying sorry. It broke my heart. When I teach this lesson in class, every class at least one student can identity a friend who apologizes for everything. Be observant. Do you have a close friend or family member that over uses the word "sorry?" You have the power to help them reclaim their power. Teach them ways to avoid apologizing for things that aren't their fault.

> *Practice—Go a day without saying sorry. Good luck. Give yourself grace as this is a hard habit to break. But knowledge is power and once you become of the frequency with which you apologize for things you that aren't your fault, you're on your way to breaking the habit.*

ELIMINATE SORRY IN EMAILS

Speaking isn't the only place to eliminate the word sorry; it needs to be eliminated in emails as well. I used to apologize like crazy in emails—as if that would make me appear humble or gracious or more lovable (note the people-pleasing theme again?). While teaching 1,000 students in mega-section classes one semester, I was inundated with emails. It would take me at least a week to respond to an email by virtue of the mail volume. I was so afraid that students would think that I was ignoring them, I'd start emails with "I'm so sorry it took me so long to get back with you . . ." (note the intensifiers–this was before I started cutting them out too). I was apologizing for having too many emails that needed responses. And I'm the professor—not a peer. Talk about giving my power away.

Then I began starting my emails with "Thank you for your patience with my delayed response" after which I succinctly addressed the writer's concern. The first couple of times I used the thank you strategy, I was scared to death. I was sure I would see negative evaluations commenting on my rude emails, my insensitivity to constituents' needs, and that I would get fired. Guess what? Nothing happened. Absolutely nothing. And in fact, I had fewer students question my authority. Why? Maybe it's because I didn't give away my power by apologizing for class size that which wasn't my fault.

> *Practice*—*Whenever you see "sorry" in an email, replace it with "thank you." Instead of writing "sorry about the delay," instead write "thank you for your patience." How did it go?*

Instead of giving away your power and groveling for forgiveness for something you didn't do, thank the other person. They're happy that you appreciate their patience, and you didn't give away your power while groveling for forgiveness. Everyone's OK.

Other sorry substitute examples:

* Replace "I'm sorry you're sick" with "I hope you feel better soon."
* Instead of "I'm sorry I made a mistake" respond with "Good catch! Thanks for bringing that to my attention."
* Replace "Sorry I missed your call" with "Thanks for calling."

Eliminating this one word—sorry—is a game changer. Now I rarely use "sorry" when speaking or in an email and when I do—usually in the case of a death—I am truly expressing my sorrow. Saying sorry means more when you say it less. Don't apologize for things that aren't your fault.

STRENGTH AND POWER
IN BODY LANGUAGE

PLAY BIG

Let's start with a little experiment.

EXPERIMENT ONE

Task number one–

* Sit like you are bored stiff. Pretend you are in the most boring meeting in the world led by the most boring and incompetent leader in the world (not me!). Sit like you can't stand the speaker and you don't want to be here. You get the idea.

Task number two–

* Now sit like this is the most important place to be. You're excited to be here and listening to every word from the speaker because you don't want to miss anything. You're engaged and attentive.

What changed from the first instructions to the way you were sitting for the second set of instructions?

Likely, your posture, your eye contact, and your general demeanor all changed when you switched from bored to engaged. It is fairly easy for any observer to determine by looking at your body language, if you are engaged in the conversation or physically there but mentally checked out. As a keynote speaker, I can look at the audience, read their body language, and determine if they are engaged with the material or bored out of their minds. Our body language communicates about us to others, and we are surprisingly intuitive about interpreting body language of other people.

EXPERIMENT TWO

Now let's try a little different version of this experiment.

* Position number one–sit like a boy. That's right. Sit like men or boys sit.

* Second position–sit like a girl. How are women taught to sit? What's the difference?

"I'm not the only woman who is making herself small to make others feel more comfortable." —Rachel Hollis

Men take up space. That's right. Men take up space. Part of that is because men tend to be physically larger than women. But even with physical differences aside, men tend to spread out while women tend to make themselves small. In fact, men tend to spread out so much—affectionately called man-spreading—that the New York City subway department had to run an advertising campaign to encourage men to only take one seat on the subway instead of spreading out over multiple seats. Men play big.

What does this mean for women? We have to rethink, and more important, *revise* our body language to reflect strength and power instead of fear, weakness, and invisibility. Why is body language so important? Remember, research has found that credibility—the perception you know what you're talking about—is communicated 58% through body language. Think about that. Over half of the way you communicate credibility and competence is through your body language. That means you don't have to say a thing, which is great news for us introverts. Furthermore, because nonverbal behavior operates on a subconscious level, research has found that people judge a woman who uses strong and powerful body language less harshly than a woman who speaks in a strong and powerful way. Body language communicates strength and power for you.

So how do you practice strong body language? A couple of simple changes.

TAKE UP SPACE WHEN SITTING

When sitting, the easiest way to take up space (your space—not others' space) is to keep your hands on the table at shoulder width. Avoid the default posture of hands in your lap. What happens to your posture when you clasp your hands together? Your shoulders slump together and forward with the sum total making your smaller. If sitting with your hands shoulder width apart seems awkward at first—like it did to me—try this intermediate step. Take notes with a paper and pen. That's right. Put away your small laptop and spread out with a paper and pen. It will help you start the habit of taking up space.

> *Practice*—*Next time you're in a meeting, practice putting hands shoulder width on the table and leaving them there the entire time.*

Feel awkward? Yep. I get it. But keep practicing until it becomes habit. The first few times I consciously took up space in a board room, it felt very awkward. I had to continually remind myself, "hands on the table" in order to avoid relapsing into small behavior. So, if it feels too awkward at first, try taking notes on paper. Taking notes yields another valuable dimension to communication. It tells the other person that what they are saying is so important you don't want to miss a word, so you're writing it down. You take up space and they feel important. A win for all.

BE BIG WHEN STANDING

To be big when standing—like making a presentation—keep your hands at your side or, my preference, use hand movements to make your point. If you're a hand-talker like me, go for it. I tease my mentees that if my hands were tied behind my back, I wouldn't be able to talk. Probably close to the truth. But we know from advertising research that movement attracts attention and, in this case, also helps you be big. While some communication experts find the hands annoying, any marketer will tell you movement attracts attention, so I see hand movement as a means of keeping others engaged in the conversation.

How do we stand when not being intentional about taking up space and being big? The default for most of us to politely clasp our hands in front of us like we're headed to communion. Nothing wrong with clasped hands in church but that's not where we're at. Notice what happens when you demurely clasp your hands in front of you. Once again, your shoulders slump forward, and your entire body becomes small. It is as if we're trying to make ourselves invisible.

And while we're at it, let's talk about posture. When I say stand up straight, I do not mean shoulders back and chest out—that idea of posture was designed by men for men's bodies. Standing straight for women means ribs knitted together to form a strong core. Think about how ballerinas keep the trunk of their bodies in one solid piece as they move their extremities.

For a strong base, keep your feet hip-width distance apart. No, your hips are probably not *that* wide, but we're not going to tackle body image in this book. Try this experiment with a friend who will not accuse you of assault. Have your friend stand with feet together—feet touching—and try to push her over. I've demonstrated this many times and it never fails. I push the woman over easily. Next, have your friend stand with feet hip width distance apart (hint: your hips are nearly as wide as you think they are). Now try to push your friend over. It doesn't work. Standing with feet hip width distance apart gives you a strong and sturdy operating base.

True, in most cases, people will not be trying to physically push you over, but they will try to verbally push you around and intimidate you. Don't let them. Keep that strong and sturdy base. If you're into yoga, it's called Mountain Pose. If you're into dance, it's Primary Posture.

Practice—Get in front of a mirror, video recorder, or a good friend and take up space while talking. Especially watch for dancing around or swirling. Don't do it. Be strong and take up space.

One last thing before we leave body language—what about aspects of our bodies that we can't change, such as height? One of my saddest moments was when a volleyball player came to me concerned that corporate recruiters found her height intimidating and she didn't know how to shrink herself. To be fair, I checked with the corporate recruiters. Not one recruiter found a woman's height to be intimidating and, in fact, they saw it as an asset because height attracts positive attention and even encouraged the young woman to wear heels.

Conversely, I've worked with gymnasts and cheerleaders who are under five feet tall and get confused for children. In that case, high heels work wonders when standing. But note that sitting levels the playing field. When sitting down, raise the chair height and suddenly, you are the tallest person in the room. PS—I learned that from a short man. Good advice.

POWER POSE

Why do I consider body language so important? Because it communicates to others. But the real reason body language, as well as all other forms of communication, is important is that it also communicates to ourselves. Amy Cuddy, a Harvard professor, did an interesting experiment.

Spoiler alert—watch her Ted Talk at:

https://www.ted.com/talks/amy_cuddy_your_body_language_may_shape_who_you_are

Dr. Cuddy instructed half of her students to prepare for an interview by spending two minutes being big. Students stretched out with feet on the desk, stretched their hands up to the sky, and took up as much space as they could. The other group of students were instructed to make themselves as small as possible before entering the interview room.

Did interview results differ on the basis of being big or small prior to the interview? You bet they did. Students who practiced being big before entering the interview felt they performed better than the students who made themselves small. In addition, the interviewers felt the students who practiced being big before the interview performed better than those who had made themselves small. Before any import-ant meeting, interview, or conversation, spend two minutes, in private, being big. Many women, and men—of all ages and ranks—have adapted the power pose as their secret weapon before scary events.

How much do I personally believe in the Power Pose? In past years, I taught marketing principles in a large auditorium that held 600 students. Before every session I did the power pose in my office before putting on my microphone, powering up my laptop, and stepping onto that auditorium stage. At my Barre 3 exercise studio, as part of every workout session, we practice taking up space and being big. It's a good daily reminder that we have a right to take up space.

Practice—Try it. Go in a private space before an important interview, presentation or other challenging situation and power pose for two minutes. Complete the task. How did you feel about your performance?

At the risk of overwhelming you, here's the deal. Please, please, please do not attempt to make all these recommended adjustments at once. While individually they are minor shifts in behavior, taken together they become overwhelming. Don't do it. Pick one. Observe. Practice. And make it your default habit. Then slowly integrate another one into your behavioral shift. As you become fluent and comfortable with your power and you realize it doesn't hurt anyone, it will become easier to make these adjustments and stop you from giving away your power.

For an extra challenge, get a friend to observe you in action and make sure you're being big. Practice correcting or complimenting each other. Making ourselves small is a habit. It's time to practice being big and get comfortable with being noticed. Change the habit from being invisible to being big. And remember, not only are you communicating confidence and credibility to others, you are also communicating it to yourself. Your body believes what you tell it. So, tell it good things.

THE POWER OF COMPLIMENTS— GIVING AND RECEIVING

FLATTERY IS EVERYTHING

My guess is that most of us don't think much about compliments—giving or receiving—during our everyday life. Fair enough. But compliments are useful seeds to build us up and to build relationships. One of my favorite ways to start a conversation with a stranger or distant acquaintance is to compliment them. Their face lights up and the conversation is started. Receiving compliments is equally important because it gives someone the opportunity to build us up. Yet, instead of acknowledging and accepting that we are worthy of praise, we often deny our goodness. Let's learn more.

GIVING COMPLIMENTS

Full disclosure—I love giving compliments. As a college professor, I love walking around campus, smiling at students, and saying something nice like, "you look great in your suit," or "I love your shoes," or "your book bag is so cute." I love seeing them smile and stand a little straighter because they feel good about themselves. And I am not alone. My audiologist likes giving compliments so much that she has a sign in her office that says, "Take a compliment—Please" and allows visitors to tear off a strip of paper with an uplifting encouragement like "You have a great smile" or "You inspire me." Even off campus, I have been known to talk to complete strangers and compliment them on their haircut, their glasses, or their adorable dogs which scares my city-savvy, stranger-wary, daughters to death.

Why do I enjoy giving compliments so much? Because it builds the other person up. It makes them feel better about themselves and you can visibly see it when they smile. And research shows that when we build others up through gratitude and compliments, we feel better about ourselves as well. Sincere compliments build collective serendipity, it makes the other person feel good and it makes you feel good.

Another reason I practice giving compliments is that it is a great conversation starter. Compliment almost any woman on an outfit or purse followed by a question about where she bought it and the next thing you know, you're bonding over shopping tips. And whether you enjoy shopping or not (personally I avoid shopping like the plague) the important thing is that you've started the conversation. Starting a conversation with someone you don't know can be scary—especially for introverts like me—and a sincere compliment helps break the ice and start the conversation flow.

Reflect—Do you give compliments freely? Why or why not?

Some people hesitate giving compliments because it may sound fake or insincere. I couldn't agree more. If you can't give the compliment sincerely and honestly, don't do it. But I would challenge you to actively seek out the positive and find something good to comment on. It brings out the best in us.

Practice—Make it a goal to compliment one person each day and see what happens. Confidence is gained by practicing, and practicing giving compliments is no exception.

ACCEPTING COMPLIMENTS

Great. We've established that giving compliments is a win for all involved and can become easy to do with practice. Now let's flip the conversation. What happens when we get a compliment? If you're like me, I tend to do one of two things. Either I *deflect it*— "it's no big deal, the other team members really helped a lot—" or I *reflect it*—"your purse is adorable too—"; neither of which is good.

—What do you do when you get a compliment? How do you respond?

When complimented on my work—where I diligently do my best and have earned the compliments I receive—my instinct is to give my colleagues credit (and face it, I do have great colleagues) or return the compliment. "That is so nice of you to compliment me, but the credit goes to my team. I have great colleagues." Or, "Thanks for the good words. I hear you're a great manager too." Or in the case of someone I know really well (a.k.a. my husband) I disregard the compliment altogether. The dialogue goes something like this. Him: "You look great tonight. Me: "Not really. (Add a shrug). This is an old outfit. Just something I threw on." Him: Look defeated. This begs the question, why are we so reluctant to accept a compliment—in other words, acknowledge that we are good?

Reflect—Why are we so reluctant to accept a compliment?

Why do we find it so hard to accept a compliment? For many women, instead of acknowledging our greatness (and get used it—you are great ☺), we go overboard trying to not appear arrogant. And I agree.

No one likes an arrogant person who is full of themselves and I would never want my mentees, my children, or myself to be perceived as arrogant. But conversely, we need to get comfortable acknowledging our success. Think about this—we apologize for things that aren't our fault (like taking up space) while not accepting the positive things we are responsible for (like doing a good job). Sound crazy? It is.

Being humble doesn't mean being a doormat (replying "it was really nothing" when you killed yourself to accomplish it). Remember, humility isn't thinking less of yourself, it's thinking of yourself less. Humility doesn't mean putting yourself down to build someone else up, it means focusing on someone other than yourself.

While we're on the topic of focusing on others, consider what you are saying to the person giving you a compliment when you deflect it or reflect it. You are basically calling them a liar. When you don't accept the compliment, you're telling them they're wrong. I'm not really as good as you think I am. Is that truly what you want to do? Tell someone they are wrong? I don't think so. For example, I used to respond to person giving the compliment that "I am not that exceptional as a coach; I have great women to work with." When I use language like this, I'm telling the other person they are wrong.

So now that we've established women tend to have a difficult time accepting compliments, how *should* you accept a compliment. The answer is surprisingly simple.

1. Smile.
2. Say thank you.
3. Shut up (or say "I accept the compliment.")

Now I admit I have a tough time with the "shut up" part of the answer given that I make my living talking. So, I added a little addendum for women like me who feel the need to say more. My go-to response is: Smile, say "thank you," and add "I accept your compliment."

I remember the first time I did this. While leading a workshop for women in a predominately male industry, a guest speaker—a good-hearted but somewhat patronizing older gentleman—spoke to the group and complimented me on the event. To his surprise, I smiled, said "thank you." He stammered, dumbstruck—expecting me to deflect it like a whimpering little puppy dog. That incident demonstrated to me, the power of owning up to well-deserved compliments.

—Throughout the week, practice giving compliments to people who are important to you. Did they accept the compliment? If not, gently remind them to smile, say "thank you," and shut up (or say "I accept the compliment").

HANDLING INTERUPTIONS WITH GRACE AND DIGNITY

DON'T INTERRUPT ME

When asked what skill women most need to learn, former Secretary of State Madeleine Albright replied, "how to interrupt." While I don't want to be an interrupter, nor do I want to coach women to interrupt, I do agree with Secretary of State Albright that we need to know how to handle interruptions.

One of my all-time favorite pieces of research is one that examined conversations and interruptions between men and women. Observing a man talking with a man, or a woman talking with a woman, over a set period of time, the researcher recorded that each group interrupted on average, seven times throughout the conversation. Fair enough. I can live with that.

But when observing a man talking with a woman, the interruption rate shifted dramatically. Turns out, in a conversation between a man and a woman, on average, there were 49 interruptions; and 47 of those interruptions occurred when the man interrupted the woman. Seriously?!? And what concerns me even more, is that when I use this example in workshops, women immediately anticipate the dramatically increased number of interruptions in a dual-gender conversation, which tells me they've experienced it and observed it. Not good.

Reflect—Why do people (especially men) interrupt us? Hint: some reasons may be legitimate.

To be fair, there are legitimate reasons for interrupting. It doesn't excuse the behavior but doesn't make it malicious. For example, I have been known to interrupt someone because I want to make a point before I forget it. *Note to self: I now keep a paper and pencil with me so I can write down my comment and wait until the speaker is finished. A win for all.* Interruptions also occur when the interrupter is excited about the comment. I have also been known to accidentally interrupt women in workshops because their comments are brilliant and I'm so excited they absorbed and integrated the information. While my positive enthusiasm is good, the interruption is not OK and, like men, I need to practice keeping my mouth shut.

But there are darker reasons for interruptions and, in those cases, we're talking about a bully who is trying to exert power over or intimidate the speaker.

> **Reflect**—*Have you ever been unfairly interrupted or observed someone being unfairly interrupted? How did you feel? Did anyone do anything? Say anything? Recognize the inappropriate interruption?*

If you are dealing with a bully trying to wield power or intimidate you, there are options. Let's start with what not to say. "Do you realize you just interrupted me?" seems like a fair, accurate, and reasonable reaction at the time. But trust me, from one who's tried multiple times, it doesn't work. It tends to make the speaker even more belligerent. They (there are women bullies too) are not likely to take it well and will probably continue to interrupt, maybe even more if they're vindictive. Cross that response, tempting as it is, off your list.

Here is an alternative approach to stopping interruptions.

Step 1. Smile. As simple as it sounds, when you smile at someone, they smile back: disarming a fight. Secondly, it is hard to be mad at someone who is smiling at you. A smile is our secret weapon. Practice it and use it often. To be fair, there are people who think women should quit smiling so much. I understand where they're coming from (why do we have to be nice girls when the boys are allowed to be bullies?), but I'm not talking about the mindless smile accompanied by the bobbing head nod of agreement in a meeting. I'm talking about an intentional smile to diffuse a tense situation. I want to be a nice, kind, gentle person that people enjoy being around and honestly, I like to work with others—women and men—who are the same way. So, I practice smiling as a kind gesture and will encourage others to smile too.

Step 2a. After the bully is finished interrupting, in a calm, clear voice say: "There are a few more points I need to make. Can you hold that thought and I'll come back to you?" And wait. Let the bully respond to your question "can you wait?" If the bully says no— "I need to make this point now" you and everyone in the room know that the interrupter is a bully who is impolite and impatient. More likely, the interrupter will stutter and even be somewhat unaware that he interrupted. The civil response is "sure—you can get back to me."

The beauty of the "can you hold that thought" question is that it also works for the unintentional interrupter who is totally unaware he is interrupting. More than once, when I have used this strategy, the interrupter has apologized; he was so accustomed to interrupting, and no one ever brought it to his attention, that he was truly unaware of his behavior. If no one tells you, how are you supposed to know?

Step 2b. Another response is "I appreciate your feedback, but can you wait until I am finished?" Again, the interrupter may be so accustomed to interrupting without pushback, that he is not even aware he's interrupting. In that case, not only are you getting your point across, but you're also educating on respectful behavior.

One of the challenging things about handling interruptions is not losing your cool and instead, calmly demanding respect. Self-control and finding the right words under pressure is tough. Consequently, I practice memorizing lines—like practicing lines in a theatrical performance—so I am ready when the situation arises.

Practice—Work with a friend or practice by yourself. Repeat one of the responses you can use when interrupted. If practicing with a friend, confirm that your statement didn't sound pushy

WATCHING OTHERS INTERRUPTED

Equally as disconcerting as *being* interrupted is *watching* someone else get interrupted. It's like watching a bully beating up some poor kid on the playground. It's disconcerting to watch; we want to do something, but we don't know what to do. Here's what you can do to help.

If you observe someone getting talked over, help them out and teach others to help as well. While the bully is talking over someone, or refusing to call on a person, interrupt with "Excuse me. I want to hear what 'Insert Name Here' has to say."

That clears the floor and your friend, colleague, and/or teammate can add her comment. Clearing the floor for another person also has a payoff for you. The individual appreciates your help and is likely to return the favor when needed.

While on a search committee for a prominent leadership position, several vocal committee members continued to talk while a Black committee member kept trying to make a statement. He politely deferred every time they interrupted him and consequently, was never able to finish his sentence. From my vantage point, they were ignoring him, talking over him, and not willing to acknowledge his presence. I interrupted with "Excuse me. I want to hear what Michael has to say," which cleared the floor so he could make his statement. I have no memory of what he said—only that it was important that he speak. Several months later, when the search committee was divided on candidates, that same individual—who I cleared the floor for so he could speak—voted with my side.

When clearing the floor for another woman or under-represented population, remember you don't have to like them or agree with them; but you need to support them because they deserve to be heard. And more than likely, they will return the favor and support you when needed. There are many women I don't like and I don't agree with. But I make sure they are heard because everyone has a right to be heard.

DIDN'T I JUST SAY THAT?

Another disconcerting scenario that plays out way too often in meetings occurs when a woman makes a suggestion that is dismissed or ignored, while a man makes the exact same suggestion minutes later and the other bros think it's a great idea. I've witnessed this too many times.

> *Reflect—Can you recall a time when you or someone else made a suggestion that was ignored only to have someone else make the same suggestion and have it acknowledged? What were the circumstances? How did you feel? What happened?*

Here's what you do. You need to call out the oversight because, if left ignored, the pattern of behavior will continue and intensify. Once again, speak up. "That was Jessica's suggestion. Good to know that you like it." Or point out that "Jessica said that five minutes ago." Pointing out the oversight brings it to the forefront of attention so Jessica gets credit. You can point out that your comment was overlooked yourself but what I prefer is to have a friend—your fan club—female or male—acknowledge your contribution to the group. Helping others builds comradery and group support.

> *Practice—Next time you're in a meeting and someone (usually an outgroup member) gets interrupted or ignored, or talked over, smile, stop the conversation, and clear the floor for them to speak. How did that make you feel? Did anybody die? No. Did that change your relationship with the person you supported?*

MANSPLAINING

Google, the expert on everything, defines mansplaining as "the explanation of something by a man, typically to a woman, in a manner regarded as condescending or patronizing." Talk about the epitome of overconfidence and cluelessness. One of my favorite examples of mansplaining was listening to a male colleague tell me how to sell to women when my dissertation, research, and consulting all centered around women and sales. Seriously?!?!? Sadly, we've all been there.

> *Reflect—Do you have an example of mansplaining? Why do you think men do it?*

As a researcher, I'm always asking the question why? In the case of mansplaining, I'm going to give men the benefit of doubt. In the case of my dear husband, who has been known to mansplain more than I'd like to admit, in my heart, I truly believe he thinks he is being helpful. Unfortunately, he's not.

When I can stay calm and not verbally explode with the indignity of being treated like an idiot, my favorite response to mansplaining is smile (secret weapon) and say "Thanks. I've got this" and move on. The "Thanks. I've got this" response puts an end to the discussion without an argument. The key is staying calm and trying to assume good intentions.

Practice—Which one (being interrupted, watching interruptions or walk overs, or mansplaining) do you deal with the most? What will you do differently in the coming weeks?

REFUSAL SKILLS 101

NO IS A COMPLETE SENTENCE

Let me guess. If you're like me and most other women, you are busy. You have no extra time, and you are barely able to keep up with your work, much less take care of yourself and others who depend upon you. And rest? Not an option. You get asked to be on a committee, board, project, team, (fill in the blank). What do you do? My guess is that far too many of us say yes even when we don't have time, energy, or passion for the activity. No is a complete sentence.

> *Reflect—What's the problem with saying "yes" to every opportunity that comes along?*

The problem with saying "yes" too often—especially when we are already overbooked, stressed out, and not overly excited about a task or organization—is that we risk burn-out and risk spreading ourselves too thin. Feelings of being overwhelmed are not conducive to mental wellness or even physical health.

We have a saying in marketing—you can't be all things to all people, or you wind up appealing to no one. If you say yes to everyone who wants you to do something, you wind up doing too much and not doing any of it particularly well. I have seen women involved in so many activities, clubs, work, school, and family functions that I'm exhausted from merely listening to their schedules. That is neither a healthy, nor fun, way to live. And yet, we keep saying yes.

There are several reasons why we are afraid to say no. In some cases, we are people-pleasers and say no to avoid hurting someone's feelings or we think we are letting them down by declining. Think about that for a minute. We are willing to hurt ourselves and wear ourselves ragged—even make ourselves sick—by accepting a position or activity we don't have time for, then take a chance on possibly hurting someone else by refusing.

When did we start thinking that others' plans for our lives were more important than what we want for ourselves? Even though my ego wants to think I was chosen because I am special—and face it, we're all special—the reality is that the inviter needs a warm body and we are all replaceable. If I can't do it, someone else can. Problem solved.

Another reason we hesitate to say no is FOMO, fear of missing out. For some reason we think that if we decline an opportunity, the chance will never come again. Yet this is not true. If you decline politely and keep the conversation open, more than likely if the group wanted you now, they will want you in two years so a decline turns into a "not yet."

Furthermore, when I've had the courage to decline, not only did I save myself from a stress-induced nervous breakdown, I opened the door for someone else to have an amazing opportunity. In retrospect, and if I am being brutally honest, the reality is that the other person did a better job with the opportunity than I would have. While somewhat ego-bruising to admit, the reality is a win for both.

To get comfortable with saying no, we need to reframe the way we think about refusals. To avoid feeling bad about saying no, I prefer to reframe my "no" as a "yes" opening the door for someone else to have the opportunity. My "no" gives someone else a chance and helping other people makes me happy. Hence, my "no" is someone else's "yes." Everyone is fine.

But let's be honest. Declining opportunities is scary. It can be as scary to say "no" as it is to say "yes" because you don't know if you are truly making the best decision. So be prepared to experience initial panic and regret when you push the send button on your decline. Whenever I decline an invitation or activity, I initially feel a twinge of regret. As soon as I push the "send" button on the email, I immediately think, "oh no, what I have done?" and the regret starts to flow.

But I have to say, I don't feel the regret long. After 30 seconds—albeit maybe 30 long seconds—of regret, I continue my work and feel a great sense of relief because now I don't have to worry about making time for yet another activity, responsibility, obligation, etc. Whew. I said "no" and now I don't have to worry about it. The regret does not last long and instead is replaced with peace and accomplishment for standing up for myself.

Another reason we hesitate to decline opportunities is that we don't know how to do it gracefully without burning bridges or hurting someone's feelings. Here are some strategies for declining an opportunity. If possible, do it by email. Email creates distance in the communication, and you can phrase the refusal carefully via editing.

Whether you're declining a job, a donation request, a request for your time, I always like to start the refusal with gratitude. "Thank you for this remarkable opportunity" or "Thank you for thinking of me." Gratitude is contagious and never out of style. It reminds you that you are fortunate to be considered—even if you are not interested.

The second part of the email should contain a vague decline. Here the words vary depending upon what you are declining. In the case of a job or internship, you can cite family concerns, career goals, a fit, and other job offers, as general reasons to decline. Other examples of ways to decline are:

* "not a good fit at this time"
* "doesn't align with my career goals at this time"
* "decided to pursue other options"
* "due to family concerns"

Complete the email with gratitude again for the offer.

If you're being asked to serve as a volunteer, you also have options when declining.

Once again, start the email with gratitude. "Thank you for thinking of me," and compliment them on their organization. Here are a couple of ways to address the refusal:

* Can't participate because you need to focus on work, family, school, etc.

* Decline and suggest someone else. I love doing this because it gets me off the hook but makes the opportunity available to someone who might be interested and excited about participating. And I help the organization by suggesting someone else.

* Suggest a different role. I avoided volunteering for pre-school field trips (full disclosure: I prefer dogs to children unless they are my own) by offering to play guitar and sing with the children weekly. Singing was easier, and much more fun for me, and it relieved me of the responsibility of field trips. Success for all.

* If asked for money, note that it is a wonderful cause, but explain your focus. In my case, I focus donations on children's causes, my church, and animal rescue.

Once again, close the email with gratitude for their cause and for thinking of you.

One of the benefits of getting comfortable saying "no" is that it allows you to focus on your priorities. I get asked to do many speaking engagements on a multitude of different topics. To avoid burning out and wearing out, I stick with speaking engagements on the topic of women's empowerment. You can make a bigger impact, and avoid the stress of spreading yourself too thin, if you have a couple of areas of focus (that means one or two—maybe three areas of focus). Having a personal focus—your "why"—makes the decline decision easier. The request either fits with my passion or it doesn't. And if it doesn't, I decline. Or as one woman said, "if it isn't a hell yes, it's a no."

Practice—Write a refusal email for a job you don't want or a committee assignment you don't want. That way, if the offer comes up, you already have the refusal email composed.

Think about what is important to you instead of bowing to the whims of opportunities that others put before you. Once I identified my passion—empowering women—decisions about what opportunities to access and which ones to let go, were made easier. Remember, if it isn't a hell yes, it's a no.

LIFT AS YOU CLIMB

When I make the statement, "my career has been undercut far more by other women than by men," I am both shocked and saddened by the response from other women. Shocked because 100% of the many women my age (that means between the ages of 40–80) with whom I've shared my story, agree that they have been undercut by women far more than men, and then proceed to tell me their story. Research rarely results in 100% anything and yet I keep hearing this same story from other women. But even more alarming is that many of my young, college women students also agree.

Ladies! This has to stop. We cannot continue to undercut each other and expect to get ahead. We need to stop behaving like crabs in a bucket; when one tries to escape, the others will pull it back into the bucket so it remains trapped like they are—and instead practice supporting each other. In the words of Ben Franklin, "we will hang together or we will surely hang separately." Since I have no intention of hanging separately, we, as women, need to learn to how hang together and support each other. Notice I didn't say "get along" or like each other. You don't have to like each other or agree with each other. But you do have to support and acknowledge female colleagues. Let's learn how.

WOMEN SUPPORTING WOMEN

Why, as women, do we tend to undercut each other? Two plausible reasons come to mind. In the early days of women entering the workforce, quota-type thinking was the standard. When women started working and clamoring for leadership positions, managers would promote one woman, "check the box," and believe they had adequately addressed gender bias.

Consequently, this system created a competitive environment where women were pitted against each other in their quest to become the "one" woman who was picked for management. Multiple women qualified for the position, but only one slot was available for a woman. This undoubtedly created an unhealthy competitive environment for all women striving to be the chosen one. Under those conditions, if another woman won the coveted spot, every other woman lost. Needless to say, this competitive environment—designed by men—did not encourage cooperation between women but, in fact, bred a culture of competition and scarcity.

A second explanation for the motivation behind women under-cutting women can also be traced back to the business culture. In the good-ole-days—which really weren't all that good, especially for women—corporate roles were neatly defined. Men were managers and women—referred to as "girls," when I started my career, were secretar-ies. That meant it was easy and convenient to assign tasks based on a role which corresponded to gender: the men ran the boardroom and the women/girls took notes and made coffee.

Once a few women made it into the managerial ranks, the lines of demarcation were more difficult to discern and women managers fre-quently found themselves in the difficult, if not impossible task of being caught in the middle. For example, in my office, if you were a man, you were a manager and therefore you did not make the coffee. (FYI–this was long before the days of Keurig and Starbucks when making coffee was a time consuming and messy task). If you were a woman/girl, you were a secretary or clerical staff, which meant you made the coffee. Everyone drank the coffee and the system worked quite well as long as managers were all men and secretaries were all women.

At 25, fresh out of college and working on my MBA at night (the internet had not yet been invented), I became the sole woman manager in my division of a Fortune 500 company: allowing leadership to check the gender diversity box. Now I no longer fit entirely with my female co-workers who were clerical, nor did I fit with the male managers who were not eager to embrace a co-worker who was different from them.

Imagine my shock, and crushing disappointment, when I saw my name on the coffee production list. Managers don't make coffee; staff makes coffee. And as manager, I refused to make coffee. That action won me no friends with anyone. The men were livid with me because they want their coffee (for some reason, making it themselves was not an option, go figure) and the women were angry with me because "who does she think she is? She gets promoted and she's too good to make coffee."

I was in no-man's land, literally. No doubt that women resented me as I tried to establish my authority as a manager. As women were trying to establish their careers in management, the popular advice at the time was to be like a man and separate yourself from lower-ranking women. All of this contributed to a competitive, resentful environment for the few women, like me, in management.

LEARN TO SHINE TOGETHER

While bad habits may have emerged from the early days of women entering the managerial ranks, it is important to note that the days of the one-woman-manager are mostly gone. Women still may have not cracked the glass ceiling, but more and more women are making it to managerial ranks. Thus, suggesting that the cut-throat competition to win the one coveted slot is no longer valid or appropriate. Yet many of us women tend to be stuck in jealous thoughts, fueled by mindsets of competition and scarcity.

I can state Lysa TerKeurst's quotation "her success does not threaten mine" by heart—which tells you how many times a day I say it to myself.

In one particularly bad period of jealousy, I was upset when I was not selected for a coveted award. Instead, a colleague, whom I could not stand, won. Talk about adding insult to injury. I began ranting that she lacked ability but was gifted in self-promotion and completing award applications. Clearly, I was not my best self.

But her success does not threaten mine. We are all on our own path. And her success did not threaten mine. I reminded myself, there are plenty of other awards, the award will be there next year, and I did receive valuable recognition from co-workers for my accomplishments. While painful to admit, not winning the award that year forced me to tackle additional responsibilities which greatly enhanced my application the following year. And yes, I won.

When someone gets the job you were hoping for, it doesn't mean you won't get *a* job—you may not get *that* job—but there are still plenty of other jobs. You are not on the same path as your friends. Not only does her success not threaten mine, we are all on our own paths. When someone gets the job or promotion you wanted, it doesn't mean you won't get any job or promotion—there are plenty of both to go around. It just means it didn't work this time.

Instead of a mindset of scarcity and competition, make your world view one of abundance and cooperation: we are all on our own path and her success does not threaten yours. There are plenty of ways for everyone to be successful. Repeat after me: "her success does not threaten mine." We can all be successful; but success will look different for everyone. And think about it, why would you want what someone else wants? Do what's best for you—not what everyone else wants.

An added benefit of adopting a "her success does not threaten mine" attitude is that by letting go of things (awards, jobs, committees, etc.) that I was hoping for myself, and allowing someone else the opportunity, a better opportunity almost always comes my way. Always. Secondly, if I'm really, really, honest with myself, they would do a better job than me. It's a win-win, and I like that.

When I was not named as the leader for a group that I would have been perfect to lead but, instead, another woman was named (and let's be real—how could she be better than me?!?), I was furious and angry. However, upon reflection and repeating "her success does not threaten mine" more times than I can count, my attitude slowly changed. If I were completely honest, the other woman had organizational skills I lacked and was better at leading the group than I would have been. And, because I didn't have the commitment of advising the group, another opportunity, much closer aligned to my skill set and interests, became available. Her success does not threaten mine; we are all on our own path. And the path reveals itself every time, if we allow it.

> **Reflect**—*Think of a time when you didn't get what you wanted and, in hindsight, it turned out for good.*

Now, I try to go out of my way to support other women—whether I like them or not. If others are speaking over them in meetings, I will clear the floor and make sure they can have their say. I try to be friendly in the hallway—because nice matters. Even in our lunch group, we have a couple of scheduled lunches to include all women—even those I don't like—so that no one feels left out. It's time for the "mean girls" to disappear.

> **Reflect**—*When is a time another woman went out of her way to help you? When have you done the same? Why?*

One of my friends prides herself on lifting other women up. When introducing our friends to other people, she doesn't just state their name and association. She highlights their accomplishments. This builds the friend up and helps others to know what a remarkable person they are meeting. And it means we don't have to brag about ourselves. It is much more effective to have someone else talk about our accomplishments, than us bragging about them. This woman considers her build-up introductions of other women to be her community service. She brags on other women so we don't look arrogant or prideful. Now that's a woman who supports other women.

Practice—*Read through the list of thought-changers below and choose the ones that resonate with you. Write them on notecards and place them in prominent places (bathroom mirror, purse, steering wheel) so you will be reminded to stay positive. I have to say the positive statements below to myself so often, I have them memorized. Do the same so jealous thoughts don't creep in.*

* Her success does not threaten mine
* Comparison robs you of joy
* Lift as you climb
* Elevate each other
* When one of us wins, we all win
* Supporting another's success won't ever dampen yours
* Girls compete with each other; women empower one another
* You can tell the strong women in the room—they're the ones lifting everyone else up

A friend of mine prides herself on lifting other women up. When introducing women to other people, she doesn't just state their name and association. She highlights their accomplishments. This builds the friend up and helps others to know what a remarkable person they are meeting. And it means we don't have to brag about ourselves. It is much more effective to have someone else talk about our accomplishments, than us bragging about them. This woman considers her build-up introductions of other women to be her community service. She brags on other women so we don't look arrogant or prideful. Now that's a woman who supports other women.

FIND YOUR FAN GIRLS

WHAT'S A FAN GIRL?

Everyone needs a fan club, so let's get out there and find your fan girls. What do I mean??? The term "fan girls" comes from a keynote address by Ava DuVernay, Hollywood film director. If you are not familiar with Ava DuVernay and her work, let me offer a brief introduction. She is the director of the Academy Award nominated film *Selma* and the film *When They See Us*, among others. Her directing success is no small feat given the atmosphere in Hollywood.

One would think that, after winning national awards for her directing and an Emmy nomination for her work, she would have projects flocking to her. Nope. She reports that she still struggles to get her movies made. Not only is she a woman in a predominately male industry, where women are all too often dismissed as eye candy, she is also a woman of color. I cannot fathom how she leads under those conditions. Talk about resilience. She has earned my utmost respect and the respect of others in the industry.

In a keynote address, she talked about how she managed to be successful in Hollywood, and she told stories about her fan girls. While in Hollywood, she watched how the boys worked and she noticed that they created their own informal support clubs. The boys were quick to point out the success of those in their club, which served two purposes. One, it meant the boys didn't have to brag on themselves—someone else was bragging on them—and second, it made others, outside the group, aware of the good things the boys were doing. Good idea.

She adopted this approach and found her own fan girls. Fan girls are your buddies who will brag about you to others—so you don't have to— and will speak out about all the great stuff you are doing. And of course, each fan girl supports the others so everyone is recognized. Fan girl support allows someone else to talk about your accomplishments—while you talk about her accomplishments—so no one has to brag or come across as arrogant. I see it as women supporting women.

WHY DO WE NEED FAN GIRLS?

Why are fan girls so important? I had a friend who is a communication expert and we spent a lot of time together at parks, playgrounds, and sporting events while our children were little. She insisted that women did themselves a great disservice when they cut out quilting bees. For you youngsters out there, a quilting bee is when women gather and sew together patches of cloth to make quilts. These patches were given as gifts or sold for charity. Whoa! Hold up.

The value of the quilting bees was the socialization the women experienced while sewing. Yes, they were doing something productive. I have a hard time doing anything that isn't productive. As we all know, women maximize productivity as a survival mechanism. But more importantly, the activity provided an excuse to collaborate about the weather, men, their children, and solve world problems. As a result of the quilting bees, the women realized they were not alone in their struggles or their mistakes. They knew other women were dealing with the same issues that impacted them. While talking may not necessarily solve the problem, knowing that you're not alone certainly helps.

What happened when women went to work outside the home? We had no time for extra-curriculars such as socializing. Forget quilting bees. We were just trying to survive. Women were working two jobs— one at the office and one at home. We became isolated and had no time or energy to socialize with other like-minded women. This must stop.

Reflect—Can you think of a few women in your work world that you could invite to lunch or coffee? What's holding you back from making the invitation? Would you be more likely to send the invite if you thought you were helping someone else? Hint: you are.

MY FAN GIRL STORY

So how did this play out in my life? I spent way too many long hours working independently, partly because there were so few women in business and academia when I started my career and partly because I put in long hours to achieve success and avoid failure. When I was hired in my current position 15 years ago, there was only one other woman in my department and it stayed that way for years. Fortunately for us, we became fast friends and navigated the predominately male department together. But even with two of us, it was a lonely venture, and we were easily outvoted or overlooked.

Eventually, more women joined our ranks. So, my colleague and I organized occasional lunches or coffee catch ups with a few other women in our organization that we both liked. Were we scared to issue the lunch invitation? H--- yes. We're both introverts. And I'm afraid of rejection. What if no one comes?

But I've also practiced resilience and, in this environment, the job required it. We found our courage and did it anyway. None of us knew each other well when we started organizing the lunches. But we knew the fan club was worth the sacrifice of time and we got to know each other better. Yes, I know. I'm telling you to get a small group of women together for lunch. How simplistic. I agree. In some ways, it sounds so obvious that it's not worth mentioning. But these fan girl lunches have made huge impacts on each of us fan girls and our organization.

> *"You can tell the strong women in the room because they're the ones lifting everyone else up."*

In some ways, nothing dramatic changed. We all had a good time chatting about everything under the sun. But in another sense, everything changed. Because now, the four of us had a network of women who had our backs. While we tried—albeit many times unsuccessfully—to not gossip, or put others down, topics or individuals would surface. Like the "Me Too" movement dramatically highlighted, it was not unusual for us to suddenly recognize that it was the same person or policy that was making all of our lives difficult. While the realization of the common problem didn't change the issue, we appreciated it was not just us, and we were not alone. We supported each other.

FAN GIRLS INTENTIONALLY SUPPORT EACH OTHER

Without even realizing it, we started promoting each other so that none of us had to self-promote. For example, when a new woman joins our organization, fan girls club invites her to lunch. Instead of going around the table and introducing yourself—how awkward is that?!? and if you're like me, I never know what to say—we would talk about the other women at the table. I'd mention that Dianne has a dual degree in marketing and design. And then continue on. "She is so creative—I love looking at her beautifully breath-taking slides. And if you ever need a consultant, you need to talk to Dianne. She directs our capstone project and the work her department produces is better than much of the work I've seen from others…"

Then Roseann would talk about me. "If you need sales, Jane started. …" By the time we're done talking about each other, the newbie is convinced she's lunching with a dream team. And she is. ☺ And all of us feel good because we built each other up: proving the strength in having women colleagues.

Reflect—*What's your fan girl story? Do you have fan girls in multiple arenas? Work? School? Clubs? Volunteer work? Write down the names of these women and make a mental note to reach out to them more often.*

Practice—*Instead of only introducing by name, start bragging on a fan girl's accomplishments or attributes. See what happens. Not only is she relieved that she doesn't have to talk about herself, she's also likely to return the favor.*

FAN GIRLS HANG TOGETHER TO SUPPORT CHANGE

The value and power of my fan girls further hit home when I was on a search committee to select a high-ranking administrator. Despite the misogynistic leanings of our former boss, my department had made great strides in supporting women's initiatives and my fan girls and I did not want to lose that momentum.

Fast forward to the final stages of the selection process, two candidates remained. One of the candidates made it clear she supported women's initiatives. However, the second candidate couldn't care less about "the girls in HR," his words, not mine. Prior to meeting with the ultimate decision-maker, all organization members were asked to complete surveys ranking final candidates.

I was panicked. I had spent a lot of time with both candidates and knew the fate of all women in our organization would hinge upon this decision. Truth be told, I was looking towards the door if the latter candidate was selected.

What to do? I called my fan girls—expressed my concern, and asked them to fill out the survey forms which were public. They did. And the decision-maker read the comments—including the anonymous opinions of the fan girls. The fan girls' opinions tipped the decision in our favor, and the candidate that supported women was offered and accepted the position. I held my breath until the candidate assumed the position. And I'll go to my grave believing that the fan girls' votes made the difference.

NO MEAN GIRLS ALLOWED

You don't have to like them, and you don't have to agree with them, but you have to support them.

Keep in mind the purpose of fan girls is a positive one—women helping women. We do not want to be mean girls. Nor do we bash men. So, as our fan club has evolved, we've expanded our reach. The core fan girl group still gets together.

But more often, we include more women and our numbers are growing. Do I like everyone in the expanded group? The answer, still no. And I'm sure some of the women don't like me either. But that's not the point—we support each other. How often do we get together? Who knows? Who cares? It's whatever anyone feels like at the time. But we are committed to supporting each other.

We also recognize that it is especially lonely for women at the top of predominately male industries, so we make it a habit of inviting high ranking women in the community to join us for lunch. Many times, their schedule doesn't allow it but the women appreciate the invitation. This way women leaders know they have a fan club of women they can trust supporting them.

FINAL FAN GIRLS THOUGHTS

Can I quantify the impact the fan girls have made on careers and organizations? No. I'm not even sure I can explain it accurately. But when women get together something magical happens. And I have felt the magic. We all have. Knowing I have fan girls who support me and who I support, means I'm no longer in it alone. And that gives me confidence and courage to move forward. Find your fan girls. Now.

Practice—Remember those names from earlier? Identify a couple of women that might be good fan girls and invite them to lunch or coffee. If you're hesitant to do it on your own, partner with a friend or coworker to issue the invite. How did it go? You don't have to become besties or do the get-togethers have to be well organized. You just have to do it.

CREATING A CULTURE OF COOPERATION AND ABUNDANCE

While jealousy and envy may have emerged from the early days of women entering the managerial ranks, it is important to note that inroads have been made in positions formerly dominated by men. We still may have not cracked the glass ceiling, but more and more of us are making it to managerial ranks; thus suggesting that the cut-throat competition between women to win the one coveted spot of token woman is no longer valid or appropriate. Yet many of us tend to be stuck in jealous thoughts, fueled by mindsets of competition and scarcity.

WHAT'S A MINDSET?

A mindset is an overarching thought pattern of how you view the world. This, in turn, influences how you interact with others. For example, if you believe people are basically good, you will interact with strangers very differently from someone who believes people are basically evil and want to harm them. A supportive environment requires a shift away from a culture of scarcity and competition to a mindset of abundance and cooperation.

WHAT DOES A SCARCITY MINDSET LOOK LIKE?

A scarcity mindset creates a culture of competition for limited resources. Scarcity is really another form of fear—fear of running out. If you have a scarcity mindset, you're always afraid that you're going to run out of money, time, jobs, awards, talent, fill-in-the-blank. Doesn't sound like a fun way to live, does it?

With a scarcity mindset, we believe we must beat out others to secure what limited resources are available. Under a scarcity mindset, someone must lose in order for someone to win, because there is not enough for everyone. No wonder a scarcity mindset leads to competitive, cut-throat, dysfunctional communities: everyone is vying for the limited resources. In order to win, someone else must lose. Scarcity is a fear-based mindset.

WHAT DOES A COMPETITION MINDSET LOOK LIKE?

A competitive mindset feeds into a scarcity mindset and together they create a dysfunctional and destructive culture. Competition fuels the fear that I'm not good enough. Yup—you guessed it. Another, sneakier form of fear. Underlying competitiveness is the belief that I have to win to prove my worth and silence the fear that I'm not good enough. In a competitive mindset, not only do I have to win, but others have to lose so I can feel good about myself.

First, let's get real. What are the chances you're always going win??? Yup. That's what I thought. No way. Further, by comparing ourselves to others, we rob ourselves of the joy of our individual gifts and undermine our own confidence. No wonder comparison robs you of joy.

I would extend that quotation to add, "*and confidence.*" A cheap and easy way to feel good about yourself is to compare yourself to someone worse off. Aha! I make more money than she does, so I'm doing great. I lost more weight than she did so I (obviously) look better.

While comparing yourself to others below you may temporarily build you up, the problem with this comparative and competitive approach is that there will always be someone better than you: and that doesn't feel good. I compare myself to someone who makes less money than I do and I feel good; I compare myself to someone who makes more money than I do, and I feel bad. Comparison is a dead end. You may experience the temporary high of winning but, rest assured, you will also feel the despair of losing. Trying to survive in a culture of scarcity and competition is exhausting.

CREATING A CULTURE OF ABUNDANCE & COOPERATION

While I tend to portray a scarcity and competition culture as negative, the scary thing is how prevalent it is. When I ask young women to evaluate their educational experiences—do they view the American educational culture, the one they grew up in, as one of abundance and cooperation, or competition and scarcity, I can barely get the words out of my mouth before they jump on the competition and scarcity classification. It's hard to imagine learning in a culture where people feel pitted against each other.

I've had a front row seat to observe gender differences between a competition and cooperation mindset via sales competitions used to hone professional sales skills. These mock sales role plays are video recorded and critiqued by sales managers and a group of peers. Results are posted on a leader board so everyone can see how well participants did or didn't do. Sound scary? It is. And the fear is palpable as I observe participants walking toward the room where the competition take place. But a funny thing happened as I started watching people as they walked out of the experience, started breathing again, and were greeted by colleagues waiting their turn.

In predominately male organizations, the men would come out of the experience bragging about how they manipulated the buyer into acquiescing, how they brilliantly handled the buyer's objectives and how they masterfully closed the deal. Never mind that I was evaluating their performance and that would not be the way I would describe it.

It was a different story, however, with the women. The women would exit the role play and immediately start briefing the waiting women on what to expect. The women who completed the exercise would share the buyer's problems, what objectives the buyer raised, how the buyer reacted to product attributes etc. In fact, the women shared so much information to help the other women, that I had to revise the buying instructions for each participant. The women worked together; the men competed.

Sadly, I've worked in organizations where the leader created an environment of competition and scarcity with the misguided thinking that cut-throat competition would make everyone work harder. In fact, the only thing the competition and scarcity culture accomplished was create a distrustful and destructive culture. Departments and individuals found themselves pitted against each other as we all competed for the scarce resources dangled in front of us. This was clearly not an environment conducive to team building, problem solving, or creative work, and when this manager left, the organization was in shambles.

An **abundance mindset** adopts the idea that there is plenty to go around and leads to a **cooperation mindset**. With plenty of opportunities for all—not the same opportunity, but opportunities nonetheless— competition disintegrates while we cooperate and help each other achieve our goals. Beats the heck out of fighting among ourselves to be the sole winner. Working together, we can each achieve more than we could achieve separately.

Remember, you still don't have to like everyone you support. I have a colleague who is self-promoting and it drives me nuts! But when jealous, self-serving, vindictive thoughts come into my mind, I remember that, as she promotes herself, she brings positive attention to the department, which makes us all look good. When one of us wins, we all win. One woman becoming a head coach, or a business school dean, or a CEO, or a presidential candidate, creates opportunities for all of us. Ironically, women tend to be cooperative as is evident in our ability to build relationships. Imagine a world where we focused on working together instead trying to dominate each other. When one of us wins, we all win.

Even if you are surrounded by a competition and scarcity culture, you can practice a mindset of abundance and cooperation and help others choose the same. For example, in the midst of the scarcity and competition culture the misguided leader created, my department head, a woman, intentionally taught our department to practice an abundance and cooperation mindset.

While success can spawn jealousy among colleagues, our department head proudly emails all department colleagues announcing a colleague's achievement—whatever it is. It is expected that we each send a congratulatory email that the entire department could read. Full disclosure—I have written congratulatory emails while gritting my teeth. Remember, you don't have to like the other person or agree with them, but you have to support them. Conversely, I am sure colleagues in my department have gritted their teeth while congratulating me. But through this exercise, we have learned to support and encourage each other, and adapted a mindset of abundance and cooperation instead of competing for accolades. There are plenty of wins to go around.

 It may take extra encouragement to get women to report their success. We women don't like to brag on ourselves. That's where your fan girls come in. Reread that section and practice promoting other women's accomplishments so they don't have to report on themselves.

Practice—Read through the list below of strategies to implement within your group, organization, or team to start creating a culture of abundance and cooperation. Pick one or two to implement. Why did you choose that strategy? How are you going to implement it? Who do you need as allies to get this started? Peers? Bosses? Coaches? Team leaders?

When someone on your team gets a "win"—however you define that for your club, organization, department, or team—send an email to everyone congratulating the individual on her success. Encourage everyone to send congratulatory emails.

If someone has helped you, or did a particularly good job, send an email to that person's leader and copy the person. Your colleague will appreciate the compliment as well as the acknowledgement to her leader. Remember—research has found that giving a compliment not only makes the receiver feel good, but the giver feels good as well. Everyone feels good. Encourage others to do the same.

Call out a person's good work at a meeting and have her stand while others clap.

Take a colleague out to lunch to celebrate working together to get a job well done. For example, when I won a business award, I brought lunch to a team meeting. They appreciated the gesture (and the food) and, as an unexpected side benefit, my visibility and status in the group increased. Sharing the wealth (or in this case, a negligible cash prize), helped the team adopt a collaboration and abundance mindset.

Treat a colleague who helps you get a win, to a small gift. For example, one woman, after winning a small award decorated the dark, dirty women's restroom on our floor with scented hand soap, matching lotion, small flowers, and scented room deodorizers to convey the concept that "when one of us wins, we all win." She may have won the award, but every woman in our department benefitted. It's hard to be jealous or spiteful of someone who shares her victory with you, once again shifting the mindset from competition and scarcity to abundance and cooperation.

If someone mistakenly attributes an idea to you—in a meeting, for example—acknowledge the idea and then give credit to the right person. For example, you could say "yes, wasn't that great! That was Emily's idea." Emily is happy because she's getting the credit she deserves and you look good because you are confident enough to share the limelight.

Help others win—after winning an award, I look to see who is nominated the following year and offer my application materials to them. Not only are the women appreciative of my help, the success rate runs high and more women get awards they deserve. This shifts the mindset from competition to cooperation.

ASK FOR WHAT YOU WANT

How many of you negotiated your first job? I opened my TEDx talk with this question. Nearly no one raised their hand, including me. In part, this is a trick question because responses differ by, no surprise, gender. According to Harvard researcher Linda Babcock, turns out 57% of men negotiated their first job offer after their MBA. Good for them. For women, however, it's another story. According to her research, only 7% of women asked for more than what they were offered. And while I'd like to think the number of women asking for more has increased, judging by the demand for negotiation skills, and the continued gender gap in pay, I have to think the needle hasn't moved much.

WHAT'S THE BIG DEAL?

Why does this statistic bother me so much? A couple of reasons.

1. As a college professor and consultant who mentors both women and men, it concerns me when I am sending the same message to both genders and getting a different response. I certainly don't tell the men to "get out there and ask for more" while telling the women "be grateful they hired you." I send the same message to both men and women—and yet the men ask for more and the women don't. While I concede I have heard stories from women students about faculty members who tell women they can't negotiate, or that women are bad at negotiation, those stories are the exception and the stories are becoming less and less frequent as the patriarchy continues to retire. Clearly, we need to do something different— women arrive on the job market with the idea of settling for what they are offered.

2. What should both of these numbers be? 100% Absolutely. Make no mistake about it. I'm as concerned about the women who do not ask for more as I am about the men also do not ask. Everyone, women and men, should have the confidence and courage to ask for more.

3. This statistic accounts, in part, for the gender gap in pay. Yes, there are a number of other factors that can be blamed for the

discrepancy between women's and men's wages but not negotiating doesn't help. Suppose Jimmy and Susie are both offered the same job at the same pay rate after college graduation. However, Jimmy decides to ask for more and he gets it. That means he starts at a slightly higher pay level than Susie. Throughout a 40-year employment, that seemingly small pay gap grows exponentially with percentage pay increases. Based on the initial offer, Stanford research estimates that the pay difference could range between $650,000 and $1,000,000 over the course of a 40-year career. Ouch. That is a chunk of change.

4. But here is the real reason why that statistic bothers me so much. Whose responsibility is it to ask for more? It's our responsibility. We can't blame others if we don't ask.

A friend of mine who was a father of daughters, recruited college students for entry level positions. Because he was a true Girl-Dad, he was determined that women working for him would be paid equal to men because that is how he wanted his daughters to be treated. Imagine his disappointment when, upon hiring a man and a woman for the same job, the man asked for more but the woman remained quiet and didn't ask. As much he supported equal pay, he couldn't justify, and I agree, giving the woman a pay raise because the man asked. He was crushed that the woman didn't ask for more, making him complicit in the gender pay gap. If you don't ask, the answer is always no. You have to ask.

WHY DON'T WE ASK?

Given the magnitude of the consequences for not asking, you have to ask yourself, why don't we ask for more? Why don't we negotiate?

> *Reflect—When you think of a negotiator, what image comes to mind? Is it positive or negative? Is it someone you aspire to or would prefer to avoid?*

I don't know about you, but several images come to mind when I think of negotiations and negotiators. The first image is a used car salesman (no—I'm not trying to be gender neutral here—it's a man) with a loud tie and an obnoxious and pushy manner. And no, I don't want to be like that. Another image that comes to mind is a hostage negotiator. I'm sure if I was held hostage, I'd want someone pulling out all stops to get me back, but I'm not a hostage negotiator. In fact, in my safe urban environment, my contact with hostages and hostage negotiators is thankfully nil. They must be incredibly brave people, but that's not me.

Because of these negative or frightening connotations, I don't even like to use the word "negotiation." It pulls up too many negative images in my mind. Instead, I like to call it what is it—ask for what you want. OK. I can do that. Asking for what I want sounds much more reasonable than negotiating but the end result is the same. You ask for more.

There are multiple other reasons why we don't ask. And full disclosure: I didn't negotiate my first job. I didn't negotiate my second job. Or even my third job. In fact, I didn't even negotiate my current job. I was just grateful, and thought it was a miracle, the organization was willing to hire me. Clearly, I was hired before I learned this material. Now I negotiate everything.

AFRAID OF BEING TOLD NO

When I ask women why don't we ask for more, I get several responses. First? We're afraid of rejection. That's right. Fear of rejection comes up again. Who likes being told no? Not me. And not many other people like being told no either.

But this is where we go back to an exercise from earlier in this journal. Remember when I asked you to find a partner and ask for $20 three times? My guess is that you were told no. Three times. That's three times of rejection. Yet you're still breathing, your heart is still beating, and the sun is still shining—even if it's behind clouds. The point is, no one dies from being told no. And if you've practiced becoming resilient, you hear "no" and move on.

We need to adopt the same mindset when asking for what we want. What's the worst that can happen? They say no. You're no worse off than you were when you started. Nobody dies and you move on. And trust me, you'll feel better because you stood up for yourself and you asked. More on that later.

WE DON'T DESERVE TO ASK FOR MORE

Another reason we don't ask for more is that we don't think we deserve it. That's right—we don't believe we're worthy or deserving of more. As previously mentioned, I was always so shocked that my current organization wanted to hire me, I was scared to death to ask for more. And, judging from the women I work with, I am not alone.

In fact, thinking you're not worthy enough to ask for more is a common reason why young women beginning their careers don't ask. In a misguided version of humility—friendly reminder: humility isn't thinking less of yourself, it's thinking of yourself less—newly minted graduates tend to focus on what they lack: not enough work experience, not enough education, not enough information about the company and the list of "not enough . . ." goes on and on.

In fact, I have heard from women I mentor that they have been strongly discouraged from negotiating. One example was a design program—heavily dominated by women but led by men—that forbade graduates from negotiating internships and jobs. It drives me nuts.

And here's why. If you're not good enough now—just as you are—to ask for more, when *will* you be good enough? The answer is never. In this example, dissuading students and new graduates—mostly women—from negotiating sends the message that they're not good enough. And we will spend years trying to drown out that self-defeating tape.

I always figured that at "the next step"—whatever that was—I would be good enough to ask for more. I got an MBA. Still didn't feel good enough to ask for more than what was offered. Then I got a PhD. Nope—not good enough yet. Or a PhD with pages of publications and business experience. You guessed it—still not good enough. My question to you is this: if you don't feel good enough now to ask for more, when will you feel good enough? The answer? Never. That's why you need to practice asking for more now. Will you get it? Maybe. Maybe not. But you start practicing now. If you don't ask, the answer is always no.

WHAT WILL THEY THINK OF ME?

And of course, many of us fear what others may think of us if we ask for more. People-pleasing rears its ugly head again. Seriously. Women are especially concerned that we will be perceived as greedy or rude or ungrateful if we ask for more. And who wants other people to think of them as arrogant or greedy? Not me. But this is faulty thinking.

There's another way to reframe this fear of appearing greedy or ungrateful. Research shows that women negotiate better when negotiating on behalf of someone else than when negotiating for themselves. That should come as no surprise. Women are often conditioned and encouraged more so than men to be caring and sacrifice themselves for others. We love to help and we love to help others. And if it costs us? We help anyway. It is one of our strengths so it comes as no surprise that research corroborates what I've observed and experienced: women negotiate better for others.

I first experienced this when working for a woman department head. I watched her continually push for me—better pay, better title, better office, etc. She worked tirelessly to make sure her people were taken care of and were given all and more than they were entitled to. But when it came to asking the same for herself, she fell short. It was so frustrating to watch her get overlooked for pay increases, awards and other perks because she did not advocate on her own behalf. How many mothers go without so their children can have what they need? Same behavior plays out in the business world.

And I too, have behaved in a similar pattern. When an unthinkable tragedy hit my family, it fell on my shoulders to negotiate a settlement for my sister (now widowed) and her children with a Fortune 500 company. The company and I haggled over the course of months, as I tried to reach a settlement so that my sister and her children would be able to live without her husband's income. Many times, I came home to my husband, mentally and emotionally exhausted, and exclaimed that if the money was for me, I'd accept the offer and be done with it.

But the money was not for me. It was for my beloved sister, who had suffered much, and for her children, who were now fatherless. And so, I persisted. And persisted. And my sister and her children will never have to worry about money. But I would never have negotiated so hard for so long, if the money had been for me. I would have quit earlier and settled for less.

REFRAME YOUR THINKING

Here's how you turn this self-limiting "I-don't-want-to-appear-greedy" thinking around. Instead of thinking about how you would benefit from the negotiation, think about how others would benefit. If you make more money, that means more money for your family and more money you can use to help others. If you are able to negotiate a remote work day, that means you can run the wash while you answer emails and that means more time with your family.

Think about how your negotiation helps other women. When one of us wins, we all win. When one of us asks for more, women who negotiate become the norm instead of the exception. One of my colleagues, a skillful lawyer and master of negotiation proclaims, "If you can't do it for yourself, do it for the women coming up behind you." But I'd still like you to get comfortable doing it for yourself.

WHAT IF THEY WITHDRAW THE OFFER?

Finally, another real concern about negotiating, especially for first-time job offers, is that the company will change its mind and rescind the offer. That's right. We're afraid that by asking for more, the company will decide that they no longer want us as an employee and rescind the offer. And yes, I'll admit, that thought has crossed my mind. However, in my experience coaching hundreds of women to negotiate, never has an offer been rescinded.

A couple of very practical reasons why this is an unrealistic fear. First, timing is everything. You wait to negotiate until you have the offer. It's like the engagement that leads up to marriage. You wait until they want you—they've given you an offer, hopefully in writing—and you make it clear you want them. Remember, this is negotiating 101—I don't play games like getting an alternative offer to play off the first offer. Second, you always negotiate from a position of gratitude. Thank you for this amazing offer. I'm excited to work at your firm and I was hoping. . . . You make it clear that you want them.

The fear, however, that the offer might disappear runs deep. I was consulting with women in a large firm whose main ask was the opportunity to work remotely one or two days a week. This was before times had changed. Working remotely even one day a week was rarely an option. Asking to work from home a couple of days a week was a scary ask. The women expressed fear that they would lose their jobs.

While I understand their fear, I cautioned them to step back a minute and consider their ask. They were not demanding to work remotely, nor were they threatening to leave if they couldn't work remotely. They merely wanted to start the discussion of a remote workday possibility. When framed as a discussion, the ask become less threatening and yes, after much discussion, they got the remote workday, long before it became the norm. So, cross off the fear that the offer will be taken off the table.

I know, I'm sounding like a broken record. Fear—fear of failure, fear of what people will think, fear of what might happen, etc. etc. etc. is the theme that keeps us paralyzed. But now you have resilience strategies and have practiced failing so that you know that failure is not the end; it's merely a speedbump to get over.

THE DANGER OF NOT ASKING

I am adamant about urging you to ask for what you want because the consequences of NOT asking for what you want, are far worse than a possible rejection. For years, as I stifled my desires and kept my mouth shut to avoid upsetting anyone, causing conflict, or facing rejection, I thought I was doing everyone a favor by staying quiet. Nothing could be further from the truth, and in fact, I paid for my self-imposed silence dearly.

While I thought I had buried my desires and they had gone away, in fact, they never went away. Like dirty gym socks in a closed up, hot car,

my unspoken desires were simmering and smoldering. And like a volcano, those pent-up feelings—that I thought had disappeared—were
ready to detonate at a moment's notice. Consequently, I would explode
at the smallest infraction—totally unaware that the current incident
wasn't really the issue, it was my resentment surfacing. Unexpressed
desires can also breed a host of negative feelings including resentment,
anger and cynicism: none of which are good for mental health or organization morale. And to make things worse, the person on the receiving
end of the emotional explosion or passive aggressive behavior has no
idea why you're upset because you didn't ask for anything.

Let me give you a somewhat humorous example of how I practiced
asking for what I wanted and the benefits of asking—regardless of the
outcome. We've already established that I am a chicken when it comes to
taking risks or speaking up about what I want. Consequently, I practice
in the safest place and with the safest person I know: my husband. For
the record, we've been married almost 50 years and decided long ago
that we were going to stick it out together. When I make a simple ask, I'm
fairly sure—actually totally confident—there will be no repercussions
from asking. But that doesn't mean I always ask for what I want.

Like other working mothers, I can use all the help around the house
I can get. Yet, for reasons that really make no sense when I write them
down, I tend to do much of the work around the house myself. (I probably need to re-read the section on control and delegating). In my
afraid-to-ask-for-what-I-want mode, I would announce to my family
that "the dishes in the dishwasher are clean." Now it doesn't take a PhD,
which my husband has, by the way, to figure out what I want.

Everyone knows that when I say "the dishes in the dishwasher are
clean," that what I really mean is "Can someone unload the dishwasher?"
Duh. What part of announcing clean dishes do you not understand???
But family members, including my husband, would nod in acknowledgment and continue whatever it was that they were doing: oblivious
to my veiled request. Then I'd start grumbling about the lack of help
around the house and put the clean dishes away as I start my pity party
about being the only one in the house who does all the work. Cue the
mournful violins, please.

One day, as the dishwasher was nearing the end of its cycle, I realized that since I was coaching other women to ask for what they want, I
needed to step up, face my fear, and do the same thing. So, I took a deep

breath, and asked my husband if he could please unload the dishwasher. I held my breath because I expected the roof to cave in. Not because my husband was selfish or not amenable to helping, but because I was so afraid to ask for help.

Keep in mind, the lack of help is not his issue. My husband is not a jerk. It is my issue; it is my responsibility. It's not fair to hold someone else accountable for something you did not ask for. As I held my breath awaiting his response, he says, "Sure. Can it wait until halftime?" I just about fell over. You mean all these years I was dropping hints and getting no response and all I had to do was ask? Who knew? But this simple act reinforced the importance of asking and not assuming.

Just do it: ask. I don't know if you'll get what you want or not. Maybe you'll get some of it, but not all of it. But if you don't ask, you will regret it and you, and those around you, will feel the pain of not asking. It is important to ask, for your own mental health. And the biggest surprise of all? Who knows? You might get what you ask for.

NEGOTIATION FRAMEWORK

Even though I was too scared to negotiate, that didn't keep me from reading books and articles on negotiation. I quickly picked up the terminology of the "win–win" perspective of negotiation. That sat well with me. Instead of winner and loser—and of course, I was always afraid I'd be the loser—the concept of two winners sounded nice even though I had no clue what it meant.

Years ago, Stephen Covey developed a compelling framework of negotiation. While his work was not specifically intended for women, his framework was so revealing that I wondered if he knew me. It explains why women are often so repelled by the thought of negotiating and why we adopt a losing strategy. That's right. A losing strategy. Who would negotiate from a "I lose/you win" position? Turns out, I did. And so do many of the women I coach. Let me explain.

	NO RISK	YES RISK
YES EMPATHY	#4 I LOSE/YOU WIN	#2 I WIN/YOU WIN
NO EMPATHY	#1 I LOSE/YOU LOSE	#3 YOU LOSE/I WIN

Note the qualities reflected along the two axes. Covey called the horizontal axis, courage; I call it risk. Why? Because women, including me, are often not fond of taking risks. We've seen it throughout this guide-book and we see it in life. I don't like taking risks and I don't even like the word risk. Yet I acknowledge that asking for what you want requires that you take a risk. You might be told no. Low risk, or risk avoidance, is where I live. Just call me a chicken. Having the courage to take a risk is what I practice to become. Take a deep breath, feel the fear, and move forward anyway.

Covey calls the vertical axis "consideration;" I renamed it empathy. And face it, many women excel at empathy. We are good at thinking about how other people feel. And honestly, sometimes we are too good at taking on the feelings of others. There are times in my life I've been crushed by empathy-overload where I've taken on the burden of feeling others' pain. As if that would help. But on the positive side, women are encouraged to be empathetic. In this model, there is high empathy—I care about others—and low empathy—I don't give a flying f--- about other people. A bit extreme, but you get the point.

NEGOTIATION QUADRANTS

Keep in mind, marketers love quadrants. I smile whenever I see one. The short coming of a quadrant, however, is that one of the quads—usually the low-low—is irrelevant. In the case of the negotiation quadrant, no one wants to be in quadrant #1: the lose-lose quad. I lose. You lose. We all lose. What is the point? Cross quadrant #1 off your list.

Conversely, the place where we are headed, and want to end up, is the #2 win-win quadrant. If you've done any reading at all on negoti-ation, you've heard the phrase, "get to the win-win" meaning the place where both parties get, at least in part, what they want. I agree—that's where we want to get, but most of us don't start out there.

That leaves two quadrants left. Take a look at quadrant #3—I win/you lose. And if you want sound effects, add a "na na boo boo" or "na na na, na na na, hey, hey, good-bye." This quadrant represents the ste-reotypical negotiator that leaves a bad taste in our mouths and is the reason I avoided the possibility of negotiating for years because I didn't want to be this person.

This is the short-term, short-sighted version of negotiating. I win; you lose. These people are high on courage and are not afraid to ask for the moon. But they are low on empathy and couldn't care less about your needs. This is a classic bully approach. Yes—you (the bully) gets the win. But this is short sighted. As the saying goes, "Fool me once, shame on you. Fool me twice, shame on me." I may be stuck negotiating with a bully the first time, but you'd better believe I'm not coming back. I don't know about you, but I don't aspire to become one of Wall Street's toughest deal makers. I just want to be able to ask for what I want.

That leaves with quadrant #4: I lose-you win. When I first saw the title of this quadrant, my initial thought was who in the world would approach negotiation from a losing perspective. That's crazy. But as I started learning more about the "I lose-you win" people, I realized Covey was writing about me.

People in this quadrant are high on empathy. They care about other people. That describes many women—which can be good and bad. I've been in minor negotiation situations—like negotiating the price of mattress, for example (yes, you can negotiate retail) and been so concerned about the well-being of the salesperson and their ability to make a commission to feed their family, that I end up negotiating on their behalf. While that is generous of me, it is also foolish and unnecessary and is an example of over-empathizing.

But in addition to being high empathy, quadrant #4 dwellers are low on courage—aka chickens. Describes me perfectly. I care deeply about others and yet am afraid to ask for what I want. If courage is feeling the fear and moving forward anyway, lack of courage is, once again, being stymied by fear.

THE I LOSE/YOU WIN QUADRANT

Let's get to know these quadrant #4 people—which is probably most of us reading this book—better. See if some of these descriptions sound familiar—both in practice and from earlier readings in this book.

People in the "I lose-you win" quadrant tend to be people-pleasers. Sound familiar? We're so intent upon making sure that we make everyone happy, we totally ignore what we want or need and succumb to their desires. We're essentially saying, "It doesn't matter what I want. I want you to be happy so we'll do whatever you want." Thud. Do you love me now? Maybe they do, but you just ignored your needs and wants and gave them away.

The "I lose/you win" people have a misguided definition of humility. In our convoluted thinking, we falsely believe that the other person and their desires, are more important than us, so we acquiesce to them. It's like we're saying, "You are so much more important, smart, significant, fill-in-the-blank, than I am, I'm not worthy to have a say." Ugh. Asking for what you want has nothing to do with humility. If you don't think enough of yourself to value what you want (which in itself, breaks my heart), ask for more because it will benefit those around you. Another way to reframe this one is to remember, when one of us asks, we all ask. If you can't ask for yourself, ask for others.

A third characteristic of people in this quadrant is that they will do anything to keep the peace. Ouch. This is me. I am non-confrontational. I do not like to argue or debate and I will do almost anything to keep the peace, including laying aside my needs/wants to avoid the possibility of a conflict. It's like saying, "It doesn't matter what I want, it only matters what you want, so we'll do that. I don't want to argue, we'll do what you want." Seems to me I've used this false belief to justify family decisions that really don't align with what I want, but I go along with them to avoid conflict. The joke is that this doesn't really avoid conflict—it leads to the stifled feelings that explode when least expected. Thank goodness I'm getting better at expressing my needs. Much less conflict than a volcano explosion.

Finally, people in the "I lose, you win" category lack the courage to ask. Keep in mind, quadrant four people are high in empathy and low in courage. The end result is that we feel as if our feelings, needs, and wants are not worthy. Hence, I'll not ask. There are many things that make us feel not worthy—I'm not as important, as educated, as old, as valued as you are, so I don't think I'm worthy to ask. The simple answer is yes you are. You are worthy and you have a right to ask. Once, again, no guarantees that you will get it, but you have a right to ask.

Reflect—Which one of these descriptions tends to trip you up when asking for what you want?

So, what do we do now? I never present a problem without offering a possible solution and encouraging others to develop solutions. We can debate about problems until we're out of breath. I'm more concerned with fixing it. What follows are strategies to help you ask for what you want.

I've tried to include various scenarios, although the bulk of recommendations will focus around negotiating the pay for a first job. Keep in mind, however, these same strategies can be used to ask for a project, get off a project, request remote work, ask for flex time, and the list goes on. Like the resilience strategies, I use different ones at different times. But I have used them all. I offer multiple strategies so you can choose the ones that fit you and your style, the best.

TIMING IS EVERYTHING

The most important thing when negotiating your first job is to get the timing right. Many young women, in their efforts to be sincere and honest—both admirable traits—have the tendency to ask for what they want too early in the job application process. For example, in the early interview rounds, one woman asked about the possibility of delaying the start date due to her sister's wedding she, justifiably, didn't want to miss. No problem in asking and this is a reasonable request. But it was too early in the game to negotiate.

When do you negotiate? After they've offered you the job. And not before. In the process of making a sale—and face it, getting a job is selling yourself—there is a process of steps you need to take before actually closing the sale. The same is true with landing a job. You find potential employers; you go through a series of interviews where they determine if they like you and you like them. Then, if things go well, you get a job offer. And if you want them, like they want you—now is the time you can ask for what you want. Not before.

Why is it important to wait until you have the offer and until you know this is the job you want? You need commitment. When they offer you a position, the company is committed to you. Thus, these negotiation strategies are applicable assuming you want the job.

I'm sure there are hard-core, ruthless negotiators (think the "I win/ you lose" type) who will play games and secure an offer so they can use that as leverage to get a better offer elsewhere. Good for them. If that's you, stop reading. I don't play games and that's not what I teach. I'm working under the assumption that they want you and you want them. If you want to play games, get another book.

STEP 1: POWER UP

The first step in asking for what you want is to recall your strength. Before you open your mouth or send that email response to their offer, get your power pose on. Seriously. I am such a chicken, I power pose throughout the day to remind myself of my strength and power. And remember—that's shared power—creating abundance and cooperation—not traditional forms of power over others. While you're power posing, remember your successes. The times when you spoke up even though you were afraid, finished the race while exhausted, created a hasty presentation that was not perfect but good enough. The point is, you want to start the ask from a position of strength.

STEP 2: ASK FROM A POSITION OF GRATITUDE

This starting step is critical and was a game changer when I came to reframing the concept of asking for more. I love being grateful. Not that I'm always able to do that, but I find gratitude gets me out of pity parties, depressive funks, and selfishness. I'm a better person, even in the midst of struggles, when I realize I have much to be grateful for.

My philosophy for negotiating is to "be grateful and ask for what you want." My hero, Abby Wambach, puts it more bluntly, "Be grateful for what you have and demand what you deserve." While I love Abby's ambition—which likely accounts for why she is an Olympic medalist and I'm not—I'm not comfortable demanding. I've demanded before and ended up feeling selfish—too much like the "I win/you lose." But I am comfortable discussing what I need, listening to what you need, and problem-solving to find create opportunities for both. In short, engaging in "yes, and" thinking.

STEP 3: BE CREATIVE AND THINK ABOUT WHAT YOU REALLY WANT

Yes, I know. We all want more money. And I agree. Money may not buy happiness, but it does pay off school loans and buy health insurance. And nothing bad happens when women have money. Amen. Preach it, sister. More on women and money later.

For now, in addition to money, when negotiating a job, be creative about other aspects of the position that would make it more appealing to you. True, more money may provide an incentive, but there are other things to ask for in addition to, or as an alternative, to money. For example, you can ask for flex work, remote work, a sabbatical, a new project, get off a project, presentation opportunity, education support, conference attendance, pet insurance (yes—many companies provide pet insurance as a benefit these days. Our dogs are all "owned" by my daughter because she has pet insurance), a title, a special office, and the list goes on. The point is to define what brings happiness to you—not what you're supposed to ask for because everyone else does (hint: people-pleasing showing up yet again).

> **Reflect**—*What do you really want? Is money? Time? Status? Try to push aside what other people want or what they say you should want and think about what makes you happy. (Hint: For me, it's not money. I want time and job flexibility. I would gladly take a cut in pay for less responsibilities and more time to do what I want. But that's me.)*

LET'S TALK ABOUT MONEY

OK. We've avoided the elephant in the room long enough. The reality is that you need to ask for more money. Even if the company has made a generous offer. Even if you are offered more money than what you expected to get. You need to ask for more.

Why? Because asking is important. When you ask for more, you are teaching someone to value you and that means you are teaching them to value all of us. If you're not going to do it for yourself, do it for the women coming after you. The sisterhood. Asking for more isn't selfish, it's normalizing. When you ask, the next woman has a seat at the table.

As Columbia Law professor Alex Carter tells, at one point in her career she was offered a salary that exceeded her expectations, so she called a senior woman for advice. The offer was actually more than what she expected to get so her instinct was to accept the offer. But she wanted to ask a senior woman to be sure. Should she negotiate a good offer? Stop right here.

Get this picture. Alex is an Ivy-league lawyer—trained to negotiate for others—wondering if she should negotiate for herself. If an expert negotiator is hesitant to ask for more for her own behalf, no wonder the rest of us are scared spitless. Let's give ourselves some grace. Furthermore, as she tells her story, the irony of wondering if she should ask for more was not lost on her. Her senior mentor minced no words. Always teach people to value you and ask for more. Not only did Alex ask and get more, her experience and trepidation negotiating for herself, amplified by her frustration of recommending negotiation books written by men, inspired to her write her own book on negotiation.

HOW DO YOU KNOW HOW MUCH MONEY TO ASK FOR? TALKING ABOUT MONEY

In Alex's case, she had a number in mind and the company exceeded it—and exceeded it even more when she asked, and got an additional $5,000. But many of us have no idea how much to ask for or what is an appropriate salary range given our experience and education.

Think about what happens when you buy a house—another situation where you will negotiate. Before putting in an offer, your real estate agent most likely will provide you with "comps" from the neighborhood. This tells you the selling prices of similar houses in the area so that you can know your offer is comparable to other offers. You probably wouldn't want to offer $300,000 for a house in a neighborhood where the average sales price was $250,000 in the last six months. Comps assure your offer is in a reasonable price range.

But how do you find out what jobs, similar to the one you've been offered, pay? Young women, whose first reference is always Google, want to rely on internet sources. That's a reasonable place to start. Websites are available to give you some idea about what jobs and industries pay. However, the cost of living, and consequently salaries, are very different in San Francisco versus Cincinnati. Add geography to individual differences in experience and education and there can a significant amount of variation between the job you've been offered and the salary posted on the internet.

While the internet is a great place to look for salary information, it also helps us avoid an uncomfortable conversation. How many of you like to talk about money? As Sallie Krawcheck, a Wall Street trailblazer with more than 25 years in the financial services industry purports, women would rather talk about death than money, and I think she's right.

To illustrate this point, she dares you to ask this question at a party. Full disclosure: I have done this. Make sure you ask it at a party where you never want to be invited back. Here's the question. Which would you rather talk about—cremation vs. burial or how much money you make? Guess what we talked about? That's right—the advantages of cremation over burial. And none of us were even close to dying.

Why are we so reticent to talk about money? When I share my family experiences and I ask other women, we converge on the same culprit. We were all taught that good girls don't talk about salaries. In my case, I was taught it was rude and impolite to talk ask someone's salary; good girls just don't do that. And I wanted to be a good girl.

Word on the street is that men tend to share salary information. I've never been a man, nor do I ever want to be a man, but, listening and observing men interact, I tend to agree that it's likely men share salary information more readily than women. When it comes to negotiating, knowing the going rate and how your skill set compares with others is vital information to help you determine an appropriate salary range ask. It's time to start the conversation about salary now.

HOW TO START THE MONEY CONVERSATION

A couple of ways to start the salary conversation. Salary, like age, can be a sensitive subject. How do ask about sensitive subjects? Use a range. You know, a woman in my age range: somewhere between 40–80. While I agree that is a large age range and I reluctantly admit that I'm now closer to 80 than 40, the point is that young women know I'm not talking about them, or entry level workers; I'm talking older.

Use the same strategy when asking about salaries. "Can you give me some idea about the salary range for an entry-level employee" gives the responder enough wiggle room to respond without being put on the spot. I also like de-personalizing sensitive questions. Instead of asking "how much do you make?" ask about the salary in general instead asking about their specific salary. Once again, this is where being a bit vague is an advantage.

Since I'm a chicken, I like to approach sensitive topics via email. That way, if the other person doesn't want to respond, they just don't answer my email and no one gets hurt. For example, I was once considering developing a new position which requires a large commitment of energy and time. I had heard a rumor that another woman—someone I don't like or agree with—negotiated a release from other responsibilities and additional money for a similar assignment. I sent her an email.

Because I didn't like her and, I assume, she doesn't like me, I really didn't expect her to reply. But she did. She shared with me exactly what she asked for, what she got, and the rationale behind her request. I was shocked and thanked her profusely.

A couple of months later, we were in a meeting and the men were talking over her so she could not make her point. Out of reciprocity and gratitude for her help, I interrupted the men. "Excuse me, I'd like to hear what Mary has to say," so she could have the floor and make her point. She appreciated my support. We still don't like each other and don't agree on much, but we support each other so that each of us can do well.

The email incident gave me courage. I asked about money and comps and got the information I needed for my negotiation. So, I got up the courage and asked about money on a phone call. While a phone call is more personal than an email, it is also more socially challenging to decline when discussing money. Whereas it's easy to not respond to an email, it's less easy to tell someone you don't want to answer their questions about your salary.

Imagine my surprise when I connected with a former mentee who runs his own consulting firm. Turns out, he had just done a motivational talk at a company with which I was currently negotiating a speaking fee. Please remember, he has a Bachelor's degree and much of his material was learned from me which thrills me to no end. But I'm the professor and I have a PhD and MBA and years more experience.

I mustered up my courage, explained the situation, and politely asked, "do mind telling me how much they paid you for your one-hour talk?" I was relieved that this was before FaceTime and that I could not see if he gave me a dirty look. Without hesitation, he told me the amount. I expressed appreciation and promised to return the favor by referring him to consulting jobs that didn't interest me. Imagine my surprise to learn he was paid exactly what I was asking. I appreciated the information and immediately raised my rates. Without his input, I would have never known what I was worth.

But the reality is we need to get past our fear of talking about salaries and remember the point of these conversations is not to determine *why* did she get more than I did, but instead to figure out *how* did she get more than me? Start slow. Admire something that an acquaintance is wearing and start the conversation. Where did you get it? How much did it cost? How much did you pay for your airline ticket? What platform did you use? Guess what? Nobody dies. And you might even pick up money-saving tips. Yup. We can talk about money and no one dies.

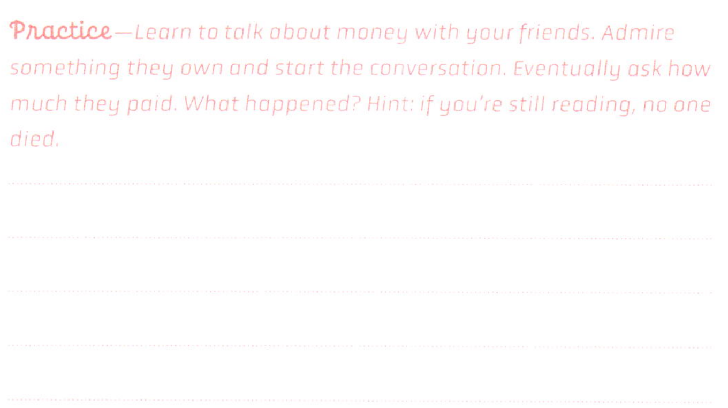

Practice—Learn to talk about money with your friends. Admire something they own and start the conversation. Eventually ask how much they paid. What happened? Hint: if you're still reading, no one died.

A favorite workshop activity that I use with groups of women is called "hit and run." As implied by the name, everyone asks someone "how much money do you make?", gets an answer, and moves on to another person. The other person can respond to the salary request however they see fit. They can give their salary when they babysat as a teenager, they can cite their current salary, or they can say "none of your business." Once they respond, they then ask the other person about their salary. Note that no one asks the other person's name or details.

The point is to get the salary information and move on quickly. After five minutes or less, the women report the number of salaries that they were able to get information on. Then I point out, once again, no one died. That's right. I've been doing this for almost 10 years now and no one has ever died. Nothing bad happens when women talk about money.

THE IMPORTANCE OF SHARING SALARY INFORMATION

How important is it to share salary information? It's critical—not just for your first job, but for your entire career. Find a group of friends you trust and make a pinky promise to share salary information beginning with your first job. Remember—the goal is not why did she get more but more important, is how did she get more. Learn from each other. I'd also include men in your group. If they're getting paid more than you, you need to know that. And every man is connected to a woman via a mother, sister, wife, niece, daughter, etc. Men need to know if women are getting underpaid. I wish I had done that when I was in college. Knowledge is power. Get comfortable talking about money.

NEGOTIATION 101

Think of this as Negotiation 101. There are plenty of resources available to guide you through sophisticated and complicated negotiations. This is not it. What I offer is a basic primer on asking for what you want. This information will get you started. Remember, the most important thing is to ask. These guidelines are designed to help you ask for what you want.

ASK FOR MORE THAN WHAT YOU WANT

I know that sounds odd, but this increases your chances of getting the salary you want. For example, if the company offers $50,000 and you were hoping for $55,000, ask for $60,000. Most likely, you'll land somewhere in the middle between the company's offer and your counter offer. However, I have to add that you'll never know what you can get until you ask. I never cease to be amazed at women who ask for more and get it. If you ask for the dollar amount you want, you're likely to end up with less than what you were hoping for.

DON'T CRY IF YOU DON'T GET WHAT YOU WANT— KEEP THE CONVERSATION GOING

What happens if you don't get what you want? Nothing. You are resilient. But keep the conversation going. Remember—it's all about relationships, not ultimatums. When I ask for more, it's from a position of gratitude not demands. A "no" doesn't always mean "no," it frequently means "not yet." Find out more about the "not yet."

As an introvert, I'm a big proponent of asking questions. It takes the pressure off me, allows the other person to feel good about talking, and gives me good information. If you get a "no," start asking questions to learn more about the decision, the decision process, and the constituents making the decision. Instead of asking "why," which tends to put people on the defensive (i.e. –why did you do that?), instead start your question with "tell me about your concerns…." "Tell me about…" opens the discussion to help understand the decision.

HOW TO DISAGREE POLITELY

Not only am I a chicken, I am non-confrontational. I do not like to argue and would much prefer to stuff my feelings away than cause controversy or an argument. As you can imagine, I've always been hesitant to disagree because I didn't want to start a fight. Shifting my language has been instrumental in cultivating conversation instead of starting arguments. For example, to voice a contrary opinion, avoid starting your statement with "I disagree." As soon as those words slip from your mouth, the other person knows you oppose them and they start to "armor up."

A couple of phrases I like to use to promote discussion instead of differences:

* I completely respect where you're coming from and …
* That's a valid point and …
* Let's explore this together. Tell me more about …
* It sounds like we both want …
* Let me share with you …

START WITH RESPECT AND ACKNOWLEDGMENT

I love these introductory phrases before a statement. If those phrases are qualifiers ("I'm not an expert, but," you're in trouble (see section on qualifiers). Instead, use an introductory phrase that acknowledges the other person's concern. This demonstrates that you heard their concern, and you acknowledge their position. You're not saying you agree with it or like it—but you heard it. People want to be heard.

REPLACE "BUT" WITH "AND"

Ignore your grammar teachers and stop using the word "but" to begin voicing your concern. Yes. I know it is grammatically correct because it signals to the reader that you are about to voice a contrary opinion. Unfortunately, in a difficult discussion, the word "but" does the same thing and before you can get your words out, your listener has been warned that a contrary opinion is coming and they become defensive. By starting your opinion with the word "and" instead of "but," you leave room for both options. Instead of an either/or framework, you've now opened the discussion to a yes/and possibility.

I was working with another researcher on the topic of resilience. Both of us had studied the topic extensively, were confident in our positions, and approached the construct from different points of view. In the old days, before I knew what I know now, I would have arrogantly dismissed her work as less than mine and cut off the relationship. And it would have been my loss. With our shared interest in resilience—especially as it relates to women—it behooved us to collaborate instead of denigrate. Throughout our discussions, I resorted to these "yes and" phrases and we developed a powerful approach to coaching resilience. We still disagree on a lot. But those disagreements did not hinder our collaboration. I credit the "yes and'" vocabulary.

"TELL ME ABOUT" INSTEAD OF "WHY"

Another small but powerful change is to substitute "tell me about" instead of "why." While "why" tends to be our default, raising that question can immediately put the other person on the defensive. "Why did you do that" makes them defend their actions. Instead of asking why in a difficult conversation, use the phrase "tell me about." When you ask me to tell you about a decision, you more likely to get my thought process, intervening variables, and other valuable information. Asking me *why* I did something asks for justification to defends the decision.

SHARE INSTEAD OF TELL

Finally, another helpful word choice is substituting the word "share" for "tell" when relaying your experiences. "Let me tell you . . ." has a demanding tone to it. Instead, "let me share my . . ." has a gentler feel to the statement. You *share* with friends. Sharing experiences helps cultivate the relationship.

NEGOTIATION TIPS

I have negotiated in person, via phone, and through email and I have no strong preferences about which form of communication to use. They all work. It depends on the situation and the person you're dealing with. Although the same basic principles apply no matter which form of communication you use, there are some nuances and strategies that work better in some situations than in others.

IN PERSON—BE BIG

If you are negotiating in person, review the chapter on body language and be big. Sit with your hands on the table, shoulder width apart, maintain eye contact, stop the head nods, and be frugal with your smiles. Don't cower in your seat with your hands politely folded in your lap, knees crossed, and shoulders slumped.

When an unthinkable tragedy hit my family, I found myself in a boardroom of a Fortune 500 company facing the company president at the end of the table. I am businessperson, not a lawyer and certainly not a professional negotiator. To say I was scared was an understatement. My knees were shaking under the table, but my hands were visible, shoulder-width apart. I looked the president in the eye and told him the amount of money my sister and her children needed to live on. I'm not saying my body language sealed the deal, but it didn't hurt and my sister and her children will never have to worry about money.

ON THE PHONE—GET COMFORTABLE WITH SILENCE

If you're negotiating on the phone, get comfortable with silence. Hard core negotiators (not me) will counsel you to look the other person in the eye and keep quiet. The rule of thumb with negotiations is that the first person to talks, loses. Harsh.

This rule has been backed up by my qualitative research. Keeping quiet—hard as it is—is advantageous. We are not comfortable with silence—just ask any rookie group leader about the awkwardness of asking a question and waiting for someone to answer. Not fun. In fact, beginning leaders and even seasoned pros tend the answer the question rather than sit in awkward silence. While I don't recommend staring your opponent down while you wait for them to give in, I do believe that remaining silent can be an effective tool in getting what you want.

One of my young mentees is an excellent example. Early in her career, she was offered a new position in Chicago which had a substantially higher standard of living than her current residence. The company made her a low offer; she countered with a higher dollar amount. In retrospect, the amount she asked for caused me to pause. Nonetheless, I bravely smiled and supported her decision to counter albeit higher than what I might have done. As expected, her new boss called her on the phone and countered with a figure, higher than their original offer, but not as high as she asked.

While her new boss was explaining the rationale behind the still low offer, the young woman was frantically calculating numbers to see if she could afford to live in Chicago on the offered salary. Fortunately, she shares my math abilities and is slow at calculations. Meanwhile, over the phone, all her new boss heard was silence. Before my mentee could finish her calculations, her new boss, nervous over her silence, relented and responded the company would meet her desired salary. Cha-ching! And she didn't really even expect to get a salary that high—she just wanted more than what they were offering.

VIA EMAIL—GRATITUDE IS EVERYTHING

More than likely, an entry level position or internship offer will come via email. I especially liked negotiating via email because it's easier to get the wording precise. Here's the pattern I like to use. While Abby Wambach says to be grateful and demand what you deserve, I'm not Abby, and I'm not wild about making demands, so my version is be grateful and ask for what you want.

The first sentence of your email is gratitude for the offer and your intention to work at the firm. Think of it like an engagement—they want you and you want them. Now you're figuring the terms. After expressing gratitude and intention, ask for what you want. "Based on my experience, education," and the other qualifications you bring to the table, explain why you were expecting the higher salary that you name. Close your email with gratitude and your anticipation of starting work. What's the worst they can say? No. And who knows what you might get when you ask.

> **Practice**—The key to learning how to ask for what you want is like anything else. You have to practice. So, practice small. At the mall, ask for a coupon. If the merchandise is damaged, ask for a discount. At a restaurant, ask for a substitution or for a special order. What's the worst that can happen? They say no and meanwhile, you build your confidence in your ability to ask for what you want. Practice small. What happened?

After coaching women to ask for what they want, I receive the most heartwarming emails about their efforts. Never mind if they got what they wanted, they are so proud of themselves for asking that they write and tell me about their experiences. Let me share two experiences with you—one woman who got the money and one who did not. After landing her first job out of college, a former mentee sent me following email: "I just wanted to let you know that for the first time ever, I negotiated my job. I was slightly terrified but I got what I wanted. That gender gap in pay is going DOWN." Can you see me smiling? I especially enjoyed her description of being "slightly terrified." I'm not sure how you are slightly terrified—my guess is that she was scared spitless. But the important thing is she did it anyway. She got over her fear of failure and asked for what she wanted.

The second woman's story has a different ending but I still consider it a success. This woman came from a program where people are specifically instructed to not negotiate a job or internship.

She was offered an internship in San Francisco, which had a much higher standard of living from her hometown. I was not surprised she did not get the additional money she requested.

But what did surprise me was her reaction to the rejection. She was proud of herself for asking. It was beautiful to watch her talk about standing up for herself and what she wanted. Asking, not receiving, was success in her eyes. Then she also commented that she felt her new boss was impressed with her as well because she asked. The boss knows that if she is willing to stand up for herself, she is willing to stand up for the company. And I agree.

The power is in the asking. And we know, that if you keep asking, (resilience), you will build confidence (by practicing), and you will eventually get what you want.

CONCLUSION

There you have it. We've come to the end of our journey and hopefully you have new ways of thinking, new ways of talking to yourself, and new ways of dealing with failure. The goal of this book was to give you a practical approach to risk, resilience, and confidence. The first part of this book focused on mitigating self-limiting behaviors (perfectionism, people-pleasing, control, isolation, and busyness) and becoming intentional about your thoughts and self-talk. If your thoughts are negative, destructive, or self-defeating, you need to drown them out. Intentional thinking is hard and controlling my thoughts is probably one of the hardest things I practice every day. But if I don't, the negative self-talk and self-defeating tapes play on a continuous loop. Do I occasionally get down on myself and start beating myself up for doing/saying something stupid? Of course, I do. But the down time is minimized as I return my thoughts to the resilience strategies we've covered and remind myself that failure is an event, not a person.

In the subsequent section of this book, we focused on communication habits and how those habits not only affect how others perceive us but, more importantly, how we view ourselves. Usually, the focus of communication is on the other person—did they accurately receive the message I sent. And I agree. It is important that our message is received and interpreted accurately.

But my emphasis is on how our communication impacts our impression of ourselves. Every time we write an email making ourselves small by using the word "just" (i.e.—I'm just checking in), we become small in the message receiver's eyes and we perceive ourselves as small too. The receiver reads the words once. But we read the words multiple times as we edit the message that continues to reinforce that we are small. When we start a sentence with a qualifier—"I'm not an expert but . . ."—and then go on to make our brilliant comment, not only does the receiver hear that we're not experts, but we tell ourselves that we aren't really sure we know what we're talking about either. We undermine our own competence and reinforce our lack of confidence. And we do that every time we say sorry unnecessarily, use a qualifier, employ hedges, and deflect compliments. We do not need to be constantly telling ourselves to stay small. There are enough people in the world wanting to make us small. Eliminating those self-defeating communication habits allows us to feel confident in our competence. It doesn't mean we'll always be right, but we'll have the courage to speak up, which is half the battle. And if we're wrong, we have the resilience to keep going.

Finally, we concluded our journey with the beauty of the sisterhood. We are all in this together and it is time we started supporting each other and working together to create a culture of cooperation and abundance instead of competing and sabotaging each other. I wish I had known this when I was younger. But better late than never. I want to continually lift other women up as I climb and I hope other women are inspired to do the same.

The men reading this book need to be acknowledged. And I do hope that men read it. Let me be clear: I love men. I wouldn't be in this position without the support of men—most notably my father who insisted in first grade that I study hard, make good grades (this is first grade!), and get into the best college I can; my husband who, with our three daughters under the age of four, insisted that a mind is a terrible thing to waste and made it possible for me to obtain my PhD: and my former department head who convinced me that I could do this—I really was smart enough to be a college professor.

Please note that none—none, zero, nada—of the suggestions in this book, hurt men. I'm not telling women to take up more space than is rightfully theirs. I'm telling them to take up the space that belongs to them. When women stop using qualifiers in their speech, it doesn't hurt men at all but it does build women up. When I ask men who take my seminars if they'd rather work with a team of wimps who are afraid to speak up, afraid to ask for what they want, afraid to take a risk or work with a team of confident, competent partners who are not afraid to stand up for themselves and the organization, the answer is no surprise. The men don't want wimps on their team.

Truly great and productive teams are made of strong and powerful members. Hence, (the title of my TEDx Talk) empowering women benefits everyone. I hope the men who read this book find the suggestions helpful. And as this book concludes, I want to say a special thanks to all the men who have taken Women in Sales. They become our greatest advocates and have a special place in my heart.

Do I wish this book could identify and change all of the external factors that cause women to doubt themselves, make themselves small, and destroy their confidence? Absolutely. But that's not going to happen in these pages. It is beyond the scope of this book to identify and correct the root causes undermining women's confidence. And while I have my suspicions of some of the causes that have resulted in women feeling "less than," I will leave it to the researchers to search out the causality and address the root cause. My focus is on helping women get comfortable with risk, resilience, and confidence.

Do I wish this book could offer solutions to all of the gender disparity and inequity in our world? Absolutely. But I've tried to fix society and guess what, I can't. I cannot single handedly fix all the injustice in the world. However, I can fix myself. I can learn how to speak up even when I am scared. I have learned how to ask for what I want even if I might not get it. I have learned to take risks that have opened new opportunities. When I am told no, I try again. And I can coach other women to do the same. The more we all start speaking up, taking risks, moving past set-backs, the more the world will change.

Once, when I was giving a talk about asking for what you want, a young woman lamented that women who ask for more are perceived as pushy, greedy, and unlikeable. She implied that was her rationale for not speaking up. What she says may be true. However, the more we ask, the less the behavior becomes an outlier event and the more it becomes the norm. I hope I've inspired and equipped you to practice resilience, build confidence, and take risks. Let's make strong, powerful, kind, compassionate, and confident women, the norm and change the world.

SUGGESTED READING

Linda Babcock and Sara Laschever, *Women Don't Ask: Negotiation and the Gender* (Princeton: Princeton University Press, 2003).

Brené Brown, *Dare to Lead: Brave Work. Tough Conversations. Whole Hearts* (New York: Random House, 2018).

Brené Brown, *Daring Greatly: How the Courage to be Vulnerable Transforms the Way We Live, Love, Parent, and Lead.* (New York: Gotham Books, 2012).

Susan Cain, *Quiet: The Power of Introverts in a World That Can't Stop Talking,* (New York: Crown, 2012).

Alexandra Carter, *Ask for More: 10 Questions to Negotiate Anything* (New York: Simon & Schuster 2020).

James Clear, *Atomic Habits: An Easy and Proven Way to Build Good Habits & Break Bad Ones* (Kansas City, MO: Lifestyle Publishing, 2019).

Stephen R. Covey, *The 7 Habits of Highly Effective People* (New York: Free Press, 1989).

Angela Duckworth, *Grit: The Power of Passion and Perseverance* (New York: Scribner, 2016).

Doris Kerns Goodwin, *The Bully Pulpit: Theodore Roosevelt, William Howard Taft, and The Golden Age of Journalism* (New York: Simon & Schuster, 2013).

Lara Love Hardin, *The Many Lives of Mama Love: A Memoir of Lying, Stealing, Writing, and Healing* (New York: Simon & Schuster, 2023).

Fran Hauser, *The Myth of the Nice Girl: Achieving a Career You Love Without Becoming a Person You Hate* (New York: Houghton Mifflin Harcourt, 2018).

Katty Kay and Claire Shipman, *The Confidence Code: The Science and Art of Self-Assurance—What Women Should Know* (New York: HarperCollins, 2014).

Elizabeth Lesser, *Cassandra Speaks: When Women are the Storytellers, the Human Story Changes* (New York: HarperCollins, 2020).

Elizabeth Lesser, *Broken Open: How Difficult Times Can Help Us Grow* (New York: Villard, 2005).

Jamie Kern Lima, *Worthy: How to Believe You are Enough and Transform Your Life* (New York: Hay House, 2024).

Tara Sophia Mohr, *Playing Big: Practical Wisdom for Women Who Want to Speak Up, Create, and Lead* (New York: Avery, 2015).

Shonda Rhimes, *Year of Yes: How to Dance it Out, Stand in the Sun and Be Your Own Person* (New York: Simon & Schuster, 2015) 193.

Sheryl Sandberg, *Lean In: Women, Work, and the Will to Lead* (New York: Alfred A. Knopf, 2014).

Deborah Tannen, *You Just Don't Understand: Women and Men in Conversation.* (New York: HarperCollins, 1990).

Abby Wambach, *Wolfpack: How to Come Together, Unleash Our power, and Change the Game* (New York: Celadon Books, 2019).

ABOUT THE AUTHOR

JANE ZIEGLER SOJKA, PhD, MBA, is marketing professor at the University of Cincinnati where she teaches women to practice resilience and take initiative in her award-winning Women in Sales course. Through her published research and TEDx talk "Empowering Women Benefits Everyone," she is a frequent speaker on women's empowerment.